SO-ARI-675

RITE *of* PASSAGE
PARENTING

Four Essential Experiences
to Equip Your Kids for Life

Walker Moore

THOMAS NELSON
Since 1798

NASHVILLE   DALLAS   MEXICO CITY   RIO DE JANEIRO

© 2007 by Walker Moore

All rights reserved. No portion of this book may be reproduced, stored in a retrieval system, or transmitted in any form or by any means—electronic, mechanical, photocopy, recording, scanning, or other—except for brief quotations in critical reviews or articles, without the prior written permission of the publisher.

Published in Nashville, TN, by Thomas Nelson. Thomas Nelson is a registered trademark of Thomas Nelson, Inc.

Published in association with Yates & Yates, www.yates2.com.

Thomas Nelson, Inc. titles may be purchased in bulk for educational, business, fund-raising, or sales promotional use. For information, please e-mail SpecialMarkets@ThomasNelson.com.

Scripture quotations marked NCV are taken from THE HOLY BIBLE, the New Century Version. © 1987, 1988, 1991. Used by permission of Word Publishing. All rights reserved.

Scripture quotations marked NASB are from the New American Stadard Bible®, © The Lockman Foundation 1960, 1962, 1963, 1968, 1971, 1972, 1973, 1975, 1977, 1995. Used by permission.

Scripture quotations marked NKJV are taken from The New King James Version. © 1982. Used by permission of Thomas Nelson, Inc. All rights reserved.

Library of Congress Cataloging-in-Publication Data

Moore, Walker.
  Rite of passage parenting : four essential experiences to equip your kids for life / Walker Moore.
     p. cm.
  Includes bibliographical references.
  ISBN: 978-0-7852-2213-2 (hardcover)
  ISBN: 978-0-7852-8957-9 (tradepaper)
  1. Child rearing—Religious aspects—Christianity. 2. Parenting—Religious aspects—Christianity. I. Title.
HQ769.3.M665 2007
649'.1—dc22   2006037784

Printed in the United States of America
10 11 12 13 EPAC 9 8 7 6 5 4 3 2

Contents

Acknowledgments

I love the movie *Shrek*. I especially love the scene in which Shrek and Donkey have reluctantly started on their way to save the princess. Donkey asks Shrek, "Who are you?" and Shrek explains that he is like an onion: he has many layers.

I must admit that when I look at who I am and how this book has come about, I also see . . . an onion. Many layers have been added over the last thirty-plus years. Some are very evident, and others are just little events that have sent me on one more quest to save the princess.

The most obvious layer is my relationship to my Lord and Savior, Jesus Christ. Next, I am indebted to my mom and dad, who have both gone home to be with the Lord. Only by the grace of God did I meet Cathy, the world's most wonderful woman, who has become my wife, my encourager, my partner, my mentor, and my corrector. Our union has produced two sons, Jeremiah and Caleb, who are a blessing to the "old man," as they affectionately refer to me these days. Jeremiah's sweet wife, Erin, has taken her place as my daughter-in-love. Finally, God sent grace to our home through Lucile Hodges, who has become my mom and my sons' grandmother. These precious layers have added immeasurably to my life and ministry.

Over the years, in the various churches I have served, I have been privileged to walk alongside thousands of teenagers as they moved from childhood into responsible adulthood. These young people and their parents have added depth and meaning to my ministry. Further layers belong to my staff: David, Danielle, Rachel, Robyn, and Brent; and Shelly, Peggy, Bobby, Josh, and Pat; along with my Board of Directors: Stewart, Gordon, Eddie, and Tom. You gave me wise counsel about the extra workload and protected me from the world while I finished this project. May God's blessing be upon each of you.

Still more layers include Lisa Tresch, who first believed in *Rite of Passage Parenting* and helped me organize this material; and the "Keeper," Marti Pieper, who has spent untold hours taking the book to a new level, including the format you now hold in your hands. Another layer consists of my agent, Chris Ferebee, who never stopped believing in me, and Troy Johnson, my "man of peace" at Thomas Nelson.

To these and the host of others who have had a hand in turning this ogre's work into a fairy tale: May your swamp become a castle and your little ogres . . . capable, responsible, self-reliant . . . saints!

Walker Moore
Tulsa, Oklahoma

〜

"WHAT'S WRONG WITH OUR KIDS, ANYWAY?"

Recently, I was talking to my son about my latest writing project. He said, "Dad, what do you expect to accomplish with this book?"

I was shocked that he asked such a profound, thought-provoking question. My boys generally ask things such as, "Dad, can I borrow five dollars?" (If you have been a parent very long, you know that the word *borrow* has a different connotation than it did when we were kids. It now means, "Thanks, Dad—say good-bye to your money.")

Since Caleb asked a serious question, I thought I would give him a serious answer. I said, "Parents today are called the 'lost generation' because we have lost the tools to develop capable, responsible, self-reliant children. I want to help 'lost generation' parents become good parents."

Without even thinking, my son said, "Dad, *bad* parents don't buy books."

Like Caleb, I am convinced that if you have bought this book, you are a *good* parent—someone who wants to become the best parent that you can possibly be. I admire anyone who is willing to take the time to learn the tools for effective parenting. You can't take the journey without making that first step—and you've done it!

As I thought about my son's question, I realized I easily could have told him that I wanted to *fix it* for today's parents. *Fix it* is a phrase that holds special meaning for me. When I was in high school, I had to take the dreaded speech class. Because I did not enunciate very clearly, people couldn't understand what I was saying. Every day before class, I would pray for Jesus to come back right away. There is nothing more terrifying for a kid who doesn't speak clearly than to stand in front of a group and talk.

My speech teacher was a member of our church, and she would regularly invite me over to her house to give me extra help. During one of my visits, she told me, "Walker, whatever you do when you graduate, don't do anything that requires verbal skills." She handed me a list of all the jobs she thought I might consider: mechanic, carpenter, draftsman—any occupation where I could use something other than speech. I got the message.

Soon after that, when I was only twenty years old, God called me to preach. Most of the people who knew me were immediately convinced that the Lord had made his first mistake. Being young and naive, I thought if God called you to do something, you were supposed to start that day. I began looking for a place that would let me preach.

The only church that seemed interested was Second Baptist Church of Linneus, Missouri. I did not get First Baptist Church. Instead, I got Second Baptist in a town of three hundred people.

When I arrived, I saw only a handful of church members. The youngest was sixty-nine, and the oldest was eighty-one. All the people at Second Baptist were African-Americans.

I had never preached to an all-black congregation before, and I didn't know that the members talk to the preacher during the service. They'd yell out things like, "Bring it on down!" or "Glory to God!" as I preached. If my message wasn't going very well, the women would take out their hankies and flail them over their heads in figure-eight patterns, yelling, "Help him, Jesus!"

That first Sunday, I got numerous "Help him, Jesus!" shouts while I worked my way through the sermon. Surprisingly, the church asked me if I would become their pastor and preach every week.

Later on, because of my experience with this all-black congregation, I was asked to speak at a black pastors' conference in Los Angeles. I had just started my message when a young man in the middle of the congregation stood up and yelled, "Fix it, brother, fix it!"

I looked around to see what was broken. Maybe the flowers had fallen off the Lord's Supper table, or maybe the microphone wasn't working. I couldn't figure out what he wanted me to fix, so I kept going.

Then it happened. The same man yelled again, standing up to make sure I heard him: "Fix it, brother, fix it!"

At this point, all I could think of was that my zipper must be undone. I attempted one of those spiritual moves and bowed my head, put my hands over my eyes, and scanned quickly downward. No problem there.

In another fifteen seconds, the same man stood back up again. This time, he started doing jumping jacks as he waved his arms, still yelling, "Fix it, brother, fix it!"

He had me now. I finally stopped preaching and asked the moderator, "What does he want?"

The moderator said, "Don't you know what he's asking for?"

The answer may have been obvious to everyone else, but I answered honestly, "No, I don't."

"Well, this man was sitting in darkness, and as you opened God's Word, all of a sudden, the light began to shine on the truth. He wants you to *not* go on to your next point. He wants you to expound, expand—open the window all the way up and let the light shine on that passage. He just caught it, and he wants you to park it right there and tell him how to 'Fix it, brother!'"

For the past thirty years or more, parents have been wandering around in the darkness, unsure how to raise capable, responsible, self-reliant adults. All of a sudden, the light has begun to shine on the truth. We've begun to understand why our kids are having a problem. It's because of a cultural shift.

In this book, I want to expand, expound, open the window all the way up, and help you understand what's going on in your child's life. I want to park it right here and *fix it!* by teaching you how to become a rite of passage parent. This book offers new hope for the struggles today's families encounter. I have some proven strategies that will help. I began searching for them during my early days as a youth minister, over thirty years ago.

At that time, I was facing a real problem. No matter how much Bible teaching I did, no matter how many activities I planned, no matter how much I prayed and spent time with the students, I did not see real growth in their lives. Nearly all of them were still dealing with exactly the same problems as seniors in high school that they faced in their early teens. In fact, they took these struggles along to college, on to their jobs, and into their marriages. Very few of them ended up as capable, responsible, self-reliant adults.

Why was my work so ineffective? Why weren't the students maturing as God intended? I didn't know what to do. I began to label myself a failure, and I was ready to quit youth ministry altogether. Their parents and I had the same question: "What's wrong with our kids, anyway?"

CULTURE CLASH

Our society has undergone a number of drastic changes. No one would argue that point. In fact, many of our cultural norms have changed so rapidly and dramatically that only recently have parents faced the truth: something is radically wrong with our kids.

America's youth culture is spiraling downward as never before. School shootings continue to make headlines. Experts blame all sorts of factors for students' poor test scores and lack of motivation. Studies reveal that even "church kids" regularly experiment with drugs and premarital sex.

Cultural analyst George Barna reports that there has been a 42 percent drop in weekly church attendance among young people, from the time they graduate from high school until they reach age twenty-five. A total of 58 percent will have dropped out by age twenty-nine. In other words, about 8 million twentysomethings who were once active churchgoers will no longer be involved in a church by their thirtieth birthday.[1]

The struggles don't confine themselves to church attendance, though. Every year, thousands of young adults return to their parents' homes, unable to cope with life apart from mom and dad's sheltering presence—and pocketbook.

While I was struggling with the problems in the lives of these students, I began to study teenage culture, and I discovered something amazing. Our society's downward plunge accelerated during the post–World War II era, when we completed the move from an agricultural to an industrial society. Young married couples moved farther away from their parents, following the lure of large companies and secure employment. People left the farms and moved closer to their jobs and schools for their children.

As a result, we made a very rapid switch from generations that lived and worked together to a much more isolated family unit. No longer could mom and dad easily consult *their* parents for advice since that would have involved either a long wait or an expensive phone call. Instead, they turned to parenting "experts" like Dr. Benjamin Spock, and raised my mixed-up, self-centered, rebellious generation!

> ༄
>
> YOU WILL PAY THE PRICE OF THE TIME AND EFFORT IT TAKES TO DEVELOP SELF-RELIANT CHILDREN. IN FACT, IF YOU ARE NOT WILLING TO PAY THIS PRICE AS YOU GO, YOU WILL PAY IT FOR THE REST OF YOUR LIFE.

Neither my generation nor the ones following have done any better at producing capable kids. The "expert" advice on which parents depended did not stop the cultural shift or its dramatic, devastating impact. The downward plunge that began in the 1950s has not yet stopped. Even with all our progress—including the advent of color TVs and CDs and DVDs and MP3s and all the other high-priced, high-tech gadgets that we consider so essential today—we can't seem to raise kids who grow into capable, responsible, self-reliant adults. It's time someone cried out, "Fix it, brother!"

PAY NOW, PAY LATER

After all, having children costs a lot. I don't mean the financial costs alone—I mean that you will pay a price for parenthood. You will pay the price of the time and effort it takes to develop self-reliant children. In fact, if you are not willing to pay this price as you go, you will pay it for the rest of your life. You will pay because your children will continually lean on you to raise *their* children, pay *their* bills, take care of *their* needs—and never become truly responsible.

You have a choice about which kind of parent you want to be: the kind who pays now and enjoys the fruit of his labor as his children grow or the kind who pays later and spends years trying to salvage their lives. I believe that you are the first kind of parent. Adding just *one* of the *Rite of Passage Parenting* essential experiences back into your children's lives will cost you dearly—but it will also dramatically enhance the quality of your parenting and your life together.

As I said, I want to *fix it* by equipping good parents and helping them become even better. I've spent years developing and applying these principles, but I want you to know that I'm a fellow struggler. I know firsthand the joys and heartaches of parenting. Throughout this book, you'll read stories about my family: my wife, Cathy; my two grown sons, Jeremiah and Caleb; and yours truly—the guy who doesn't always get it right.

Our family life has brought us tears as well as laughter. It's also helped me test the answers I found. These answers have helped us to deal with the cultural forces none of us can control. These persistent forces have cost today's parents the ability to equip their kids to grow up to lead capable, responsible, self-reliant lives. What's wrong with our kids is what's wrong with our culture. It's not just time for a change—it's time for us to fix it, brother!

Understanding the gaps cultural forces have left in our kids' lives and implementing Rite of Passage Parenting will produce change that lasts. I can say this because I've seen it happen again and again. Families who have added these four essential experiences back into their kids' lives are seeing some great results. Even in a world filled with chaos and confusion, caring families can help their children become capable, responsible, self-reliant adults.

I know you're a good parent—after all, you bought the book. I want to help you become an even better parent, so let's begin together. What's wrong with our kids, anyway?

Fix it, brother!

ESSENTIAL
EXPERIENCE #1

RITE *of*
PASSAGE

CHAPTER ONE

WHAT'S MISSING: KIDS NEED A RITE OF PASSAGE

Cultural shifts have led to the loss of a rite of passage—a clearly defined line that distinguishes childhood from adulthood.

M y youngest son, Caleb, has the gift of creativity. As he was growing up, this gift expressed itself in all kinds of unusual ways.

One day, his mother and I were on our way to his middle school parent-teacher conference when the school nurse met us in the hall. She stopped and asked us, "How is your son's diabetes?"

At first, we assumed she had the wrong parents. However, as we questioned her further, she began to tell us that ever since Caleb had been at that school, he came to see her every so often, complaining that his blood sugar had dropped dangerously low. He would ask her for a spare candy bar and eat it while resting on the cot in her office.

The nurse also told us that it seemed as if Caleb's low-blood-sugar episodes were coming closer and closer together. She was very concerned about him. We finally had to tell her that our son didn't have diabetes—just a creative mind and a not-so-holy hunger for candy bars. (By the way, God healed him of diabetes the very next day! Miracles never cease.)

That event reminded me that this child was different, this child was special, this child had the potential to raise my blood pressure.

DREAM DATE

Based on our own upbringing, my wife and I seemed destined to have average, "normal" kids. I grew up in an average, middle-class family near Kansas City, Missouri. You can't get much more average or normal than Kansas City, Missouri. I was an average, normal, middle-class kid who grew up and married an average, normal, middle-class young woman who also came from that same area of middle-class America. So how did we end up with a Caleb?

Probably the same way we ended up with a Jeremiah. Anyone who has kids knows how different they can be—almost as though they deliberately set themselves at opposite extremes. One of my favorite stories about Jeremiah happened near the end of his high school years. As a young teen, Jeremiah wrote out a numbered list of his most important values. This value system included a commitment to postpone dating until after he graduated from high school. However, he decided—in his organized, efficient way—that he would make an exception for the senior prom. Cathy and I watched with more than slight interest as Jeremiah finalized his plans, rented a tux, and made the other needed arrangements.

On the big night, our son told us he would bring his date by the house so we could take a few pictures. We could hardly wait to meet this lucky young woman. I caught my breath when the car pulled up in the driveway. Trying to appear casual, I held back on my natural inclination to fling open the door and run down the walk to throw my arms around my son and his dream date.

I have to admit it: I gasped. The beautiful young Amazon that Jeremiah escorted nearly had to duck as she entered our front door. I know she stood at least five feet fourteen inches high. She had a very mature figure that matched her statuesque height. Smiling a bit nervously, she turned to show us her elegant formal and matching corsage as our son introduced her, beaming.

"Mom and Dad, I'd like you to meet Marcia. She goes to school with me—she's a freshman."

A freshman? Freshman girls sure had changed since my high school days! Wait a minute—a freshman! Had Jeremiah lost his mind? A graduating senior, dating a freshman? Did her parents know about this?

I knew it was time for more father-son wisdom. "Uh, Jeremiah, will you come with me just a minute?" I cleared my throat uncertainly. "There's, uh . . . something I want to show you in the kitchen."

Jeremiah obediently followed me out of the living room and down the hall as Cathy began making small—make that *tall*—talk with his young friend. It didn't take long for me to find my voice. "Jeremiah. A freshman? What were you *thinking*?"

Jeremiah had no chance to respond before I continued my tirade. "Son, seniors shouldn't date freshmen! If there's not a school rule against that, there ought to be! How old is she, anyway—fourteen?"

By now, I may as well have been doing the Chicken Dance. I angrily waved my arms around, forgetting all about teachable moments.

"How did you come up with her, anyway? Couldn't you have picked some nice, quiet, twelfth-grade girl? Someone who'd have more in common with you—someone who wasn't *three years younger?*"

As usual, Jeremiah remained much calmer than I. "Do you know why I chose Marcia, Dad? I looked at all the girls in our high school. It took me a long time to decide—but I did. Marcia is the one girl who has qualities most like Mom."

My jaw felt just a little shaky after I picked it back up from the kitchen floor, but I managed to squeak out, "Uh, son."

"Yes, Dad?"

"Son . . . here's some money, in case you and Marcia need to get anything extra. She sounds like a great girl. Go on to the prom . . . I know you'll have a wonderful time."

No Such Thing as a "Normal" Child

As I said, of all people, I really should have been the one to have normal kids. What normal kid evaluates every girl in school to see which one most closely resembles his mother? For that matter, what normal kid could convince a school nurse to give him candy bars by telling her about his daily struggles with low blood sugar?

As a longtime youth minister, I should have already known the answer: there's no such thing as a "normal" child.

I've done a lot of traveling overseas. Even when I'm in another country, I keep an eye out for young people. Watching kids from other cultures has been one of the main ways I learned about the dramatic shifts that affect American families today. I would look at kids from other countries, and then at the kids in my youth group—the teenagers who seem to spend half their time watching MTV, and the other half in the drive-through lane at McDonald's—even at my own boys—and wonder which seemed more "normal." I think you already know the answer.

WANT AMMO WITH THAT?

It was on a trip to Israel that the comparison first struck me. As I entered the crowded McDavid's (yes, it was a real—and kosher—Israeli fast food restaurant), my stomach growled, anticipating a midday meal. Scanning quickly, I spotted an empty corner booth. I ordered my lunch and hurried to the staked-out seat. The tables around me were filled with the typical lunchtime customers: an overworked mother and her three energetic children; a senior citizen with his Hebrew newspaper in one hand and a half-eaten burger in the other; two loud-talking businessmen, their untouched food on the trays between them.

As I ate my lunch and continued to observe the diners around me . . . I saw them. They sat facing each other, so close that their noses almost touched. These fresh-faced, bright-eyed teenagers used two straws to share the same malt, held hands across the table, and playfully fed each other French fries. Just like back home in America, right?

Wrong. Hunger forgotten, I set my food down and leaned forward to get a closer look: *Surely I don't see what I think I'm seeing!* Each of the teens wore a machine gun slung over one shoulder. Fear gripped my heart, and my first thought was to warn someone in authority. Since no one else seemed concerned, I began to relax. *This is not the United States, where the sight of a loaded gun in a public place is a cause for alarm,* I reminded myself. *This is Israel, a country where they like to say, "There are no blanks." The soldiers carry fully loaded, ready-to-fire guns.* Yes, these lovebirds were teenagers, but they were also Israeli soldiers.

I sat there longer than I should have, watching them and wondering how I would have reacted if this scene had occurred back in the United States. How many American teenagers would you trust to carry a fully loaded machine gun in a public place?

Mᴄ Dᴀᴠɪᴅ'ꜱ Mᴏᴍᴇɴᴛ

In Israel, the two young people I watched appeared to be living with the realities and responsibilities of adulthood. As soldiers, they would have been carefully trained and commissioned to carry out their duties. Chronologically, they were teenagers—and yet their society regarded them as adults.

In the United States, however, our culture delays the assumption of adult tasks as long as possible—with unfortunate results. Parents and teachers across the country complain about the headaches of dealing with children today. We typically describe kids as *rude, lazy,* and *apathetic.* In fact, there is no longer a *normal* teenager. At some point in the past thirty years or so, it became normal for a teenager to be *abnormal.* It's that simple.

It's also that complicated. At McDavid's, I watched two young people who had already accepted *adult responsibilities* for their own lives and for those over whom their jobs gave them authority. They lived capable lives and accepted *adult consequences,* the predictable outcomes of their own choices. The students I worked with every day seemed much less mature and responsible than these malt-sharing, machine gun–toting Israeli teens.

And as I watched them, a thought came to me: *Which kind of teenager do I want my own boys to be?* If I had to choose between the two extremes, which kind of teenager would I prefer to raise?

Deep down, I wanted Caleb and Jeremiah to become more like the responsible McDavid's Teens than the McDonald's Kids.

This experience marked a life-changing moment for me. From that point forward, I was on a quest to discover what distinguished these two very different sets of teenagers. What made them different? Why were they different? Of course I didn't want to equip any student with a machine gun, but how could I bring the McDonald's Kids up to McDavid's Teens' standards? How could I keep their youthful exuberance and energy, but add the capable, responsible qualities that I witnessed in the few minutes I sat watching the Israeli teens?

I began to pray. I began to dig deep into Scripture. I began to study youth culture. I began to watch the teenagers I worked with and the teenagers my sons were becoming. The more I prayed and studied and watched, the more I realized that something was missing in our culture. There had been a day when American teens looked and acted more like the Israeli ones— when teens accepted adult responsibilities.

- ADULT RESPONSIBILITIES: An individual's obligations to himself and to others under his authority.
- ADULT CONSEQUENCES: Predictable outcomes determined by one's own choices.
- McDAVID'S TEENS: Young people whose lives demonstrate that they are moving toward capable, responsible, self-reliant adulthood.
- McDONALD'S KIDS: Young people who continue to exhibit childish incompetence, irresponsibility, and dependence on others.

WALTON'S MOUNTAIN REVISITED

While I was growing up, my parents used to make us sit through (back then, it seemed more like "suffer through") a television show called *The Waltons.* Each week the show reached us through the vision and voice of John-Boy, the eldest son of John and Olivia Walton. John-Boy worked with his dad on a farm in the Blue Ridge Mountains and helped him run the sawmill.

Today, this show might be considered politically incorrect. For instance, John and Olivia actually expected John-Boy to *work*—planting corn, feeding livestock, and chopping wood. He and his six siblings had to do their chores in order for the family to survive. You would never hear his dad say, "You know what? We ought to let our kids be kids. They'll grow up soon enough."

If *The Waltons* had been written about a modern-day family, the show would look very different. First of all, no one would expect John-Boy to help his family. While his dad tried to keep the farm going, John-Boy would sit in his room, playing video games. His sole responsibilities would consist of making his bed and taking out the trash. He could only accomplish these tasks, of course, with tremendous whining, complaining, and snorting like a bull poised for attack.

If the contemporary John and Olivia ever dared to let John-Boy go outside, he would certainly have to be covered from head to toe in protective gear. Can you see our modern-day John-Boy coming out to chop wood? He would have a helmet—not just any old helmet, but one that had passed all the government safety ratings. He would don protective eyewear, elbow pads, and safety shoes with reinforced steel toes. His parents would make sure he had a rope tying the ax handle to his wrist. That way, if he let the ax slip, it wouldn't go very far.

It would have a safety shield covering its head so John-Boy wouldn't accidentally cut himself. Of course, it would also come with a safety DVD so he could learn which end was sharp and how he should always keep it pointed away from his face. Finally, the ax would come shrink-wrapped in clear plastic—the kind that even a nuclear blast can't break free.

CAUGHT IN THE SHIFT

It's funny though. The John-Boy of the 1930s was actually much better off than our modern-day John-Boy. After all, his family had prepared him to live as a responsible adult. As a young child, he had learned that his work was important to his family. He had much more in common with the McDavid's Teens than the McDonald's Kids we know today. What made John-Boy so different from our kids? Educator Stephen Glenn offers an explanation:

> The last half of the twentieth century saw massive changes in American society . . . For our forebears, most of whom lived in rural environments, life proceeded at a relatively slow pace. They had time to adapt to external changes. But today we are caught in a vortex of technological and societal change that is whirling ever faster. Instead of the stability and familiarity our grandparents knew, we are faced with the need to adapt to constantly changing conditions. . . . Nowhere is the stress of that journey more evident than among families and young people.[1]

Families today have been caught in this cultural shift. The relatively fast switch from an agricultural to an industrial society, which happened between 1930 and 1950, left huge gaps in our culture and in our families.

In 1930, according to the census, 70 percent of all Americans lived on farms or in small communities. By 1950, a complete reversal had occurred: nearly 70 percent lived in an urban/suburban environment, and only one-third lived on farms or in small communities. And even those in a rural environment had an urban lifestyle. They commuted to work, had televisions in their homes, and had their children bused to school.[2]

Teenager and Beyond

Although John-Boy and the young people of earlier generations lived through their teen years, they were never teenagers. In fact, the word *teenager* is less than a century old. Its first recorded use, as the hyphenated word *teen-ager*, was in a 1941 article in *Popular Science* magazine.[3] About the time that our culture changed from agricultural to industrial, our country also began to develop the idea of the lazy, spoiled, self-indulgent teenager.

What happened? During the Depression, men needed work. It no longer seemed appropriate for a teen to do a job that an adult with a family could do instead. "Like the Hoover Dam, the American teenager was a New Deal project, a massive redirection of energy. The national policy was to get the young out of the workforce so that more jobs would be available to family men."[4]

As the culture shifted, our society created new paradigms to go along with it. First, we invented this new concept of the *teenager*. Second, we reinvented something we now consider an American institution: the high school. For the first time, high school attendance became compulsory. No longer could the carpenter's son spend his days learning his father's trade, or the farm boy stay home during harvest season to help his dad bring in the crops. Suddenly, very different types of kids from very different families were forced to make their transition to adulthood sharing the very same experience. When teens left the workforce, they had to go somewhere—and that place was high school.

> In a 1750s classroom, a nineteen-year-old might have learned from the same textbook as an eight-year-old. And a sixteen-year-old could be a physician! A hundred years later, the teenage girl might be a factory worker, her brother a businessman. A century after that, we would find them all in high school, and a kid in Memphis with a bizarre fashion sense could set styles for the entire world.[5]

WHAT'S MISSING?

In the post–World War II era, as our culture completed its move from the farm to the suburbs, it managed to take away even more of our children's tasks and responsibilities. The new suburbanites enjoyed the ease and comfort of their modern lifestyle. Many of them were thankful that their kids didn't have to work as hard as they had during their own growing-up years. What the parents failed to realize was that this hard work had actually *helped* them in their progress toward capable, responsible adulthood. The fifteen-year-old, once thought of as a man with adult skills who could drive and run a farm, was now stuck in high school and told he was "just a kid." Hine puts it like this:

What was new about the idea of the teenager at the time the word first appeared during World War II was the assumption that all young people, regardless of their class, location, or ethnicity, should have essentially the same experience, spent with people exactly their age, in an environment defined by high school and pop culture. The teen years have become defined not as an interlude but rather as something central to life, a period of preparation and self-definition, a period of indulgence and unfocused energy. From the start, it has embodied extreme ambivalence about the people it described . . .

Our beliefs about teenagers are deeply contradictory. They should be free to become themselves. They need many years of training and study. They know more about the future than adults do. They know hardly anything at all. They ought to know the value of a dollar. They should be protected from the world of work. They are frail, vulnerable creatures. They are children. They are sex fiends. They are the death of culture. They are the hope of us all.[6]

Many of the problems today's parents encounter in raising their McDonald's Kids trace directly back to this cultural shift and the gaps it created. Often, parents come to me and say, "What have I done wrong? Why can't my kids grow up? Why don't they become responsible adults?"

I respond by teaching them about the cultural changes, saying, "What if I tell you it's not your fault? It's the culture; and I can help you learn how to overcome the shift."

"You mean I'm not such a bad parent after all?"

Just like these parents, you are a much better parent than

you think you are. Very few parents today have been instructed in ways to handle the cultural shift. Once I teach you about Rite of Passage Parenting, you will become responsible for going back and casting these essential experiences into your children's lives.

Cultural commentator Frederica Mathewes-Green paints a vivid picture of what's missing today when she writes about the classic 1946 Christmas movie, *It's A Wonderful Life*, comparing its implications to those taught by our culture:

> George Bailey has dreams of being an explorer and traveling the world, but he keeps nobly setting these aside in order to care for his family. Nobody would make this movie today. In today's version, George Bailey would have a screaming fight with his father, storm out of the house, hop on a steamer, circle the world, have dangerous and exciting adventures, and return home to a big celebration. His dad would then tell him, with tears in his eyes, "You were right all along, son."[7]

Essential Experience #1: A Rite of Passage

By now, it should be obvious. The McDavid's Teens, John-Boy Walton, and the sacrificial George Bailey all took on adult tasks and responsibilities. The reason they could do this so capably was that each one had experienced something that today's kids are missing: *a rite of passage*—in other words, *a clearly defined line that distinguishes childhood from adulthood.*

What do I mean by that? I understand what a rite of passage is because I experienced one myself. For those of us who grew up at the front end of the Baby Boom, high school graduation marked an unspoken but distinct dividing line between childhood and adulthood. When I finished high school in 1969, my parents did not expect me to continue living at home. They assumed, as I did, that I was capable of living on my own and taking on adult responsibilities. After all, I had worked as a photographer since I was twelve years old, and was now part owner of my own business.

As we went through high school, my buddies and I exhibited some real teenage behavior, including our defiant protests of the Vietnam War. However, after graduation, we all took on adult responsibilities right away. We got jobs. Some of us got married. Some went on to college.

Me? I did what many of my friends did. Not long after graduation, I traded my protest signs for a military uniform. I quickly became a full-fledged, adult member of Uncle Sam's Army. I wasn't confused about who I was or what I could do. Like George Bailey, I took on adult responsibilities because I had crossed over from childhood into adulthood.

Experiencing a rite of passage allows young people to let go of childlike behavior and to begin taking on adult responsibilities and their accompanying consequences. One rite of passage that you may already know about exists in Jewish culture: the traditional celebration of the Bar or Bat Mitzvah (for a boy or girl, respectively) at age thirteen. Kids take years preparing for their Mitzvah ceremony, a time in which they lead in a worship service, celebrate God's Word, and share the happiness of their new adult status with family and friends. An online resource guide discusses the significance of this rite of passage:

> By tradition, because a Bar/Bat Mitzvah ceremony is a custom, not a commandment, age thirteen is when a child becomes obligated to the ritual responsibilities

of Jewish life . . . becoming a Bar/Bat Mitzvah is certainly an important life-cycle event. In secular terms, this point in a teen's life often marks enormous growth and maturity reflected by several years of study and practice before the special day. Combined with the responsibility of Jewish adulthood, this event often brings an overwhelming wave of emotion to parents and close relatives.[8]

The traditional Jewish culture prepares children for the move from childhood to adulthood by providing a meaningful Mitzvah. Many other cultures also provide a clearly defined pathway between childhood and adult living with its responsibilities and consequences. However, when our own culture shifted, we lost this key element. Without it, our kids and our families continue to miss out.

RITE OF PASSAGE

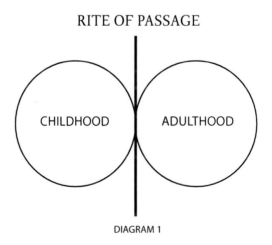

DIAGRAM 1

Even Hollywood has acknowledged the importance of a rite of passage. George Lucas's famed Star Wars series shows us Luke Skywalker's rite of passage as he trains and moves toward the coveted status of Jedi knight. In the movie *Big*, Tom Hanks's character, Josh Baskin, demonstrates a child's need and desire for a rite of passage when he wakes up one day to discover that he has traded his thirteen-year-old body for that of a grown man. We enjoy watching his antics as he continues to live with the mind and interests of a teenager even though his body is fully mature. Big Josh plays tunes on the floor piano keys at FAO Schwartz, eats pickled baby corn appetizers row by row like corn on the cob, and fills his apartment with an assortment of expensive toys (including a trampoline) instead of furniture.

What's wrong with our kids, anyway? Unfortunately, many of today's young adults share Josh Baskin's problem (without its accompanying humor) because they have never experienced a rite of passage. In fact, if you don't get a grip on what's missing in your child's life and correct it, he or she will very likely end up just as unprepared and unable to cope with responsible adult life as the *Big* hero. Because a rite of passage makes such a great difference in kids' lives, missing this essential experience means that they miss out.

ᔥ Rite of Passage Parenting Summary ᔧ

The relatively fast shift from an agricultural to an industrial society, completed in the 1950s, has left huge gaps in our society and in today's families. The false concept of the *teenager* has helped foster the idea that young people cannot make meaningful contributions to family life.

Parents—it's not your fault. Before the cultural shift, young people took on adult responsibilities and their accompanying adult consequences because they experienced either a formal or an informal rite of passage. In this way, they were much better prepared to become capable, responsible, self-reliant adults than most young people are today.

ᔌ

How It Shows:
"Why Can't You Just Grow Up?"

*The loss of a rite of passage has left parents and kids
confused and uncertain about exactly when adulthood
begins.*

I believe that Jesus is the sinless Savior. He died on the
cross to pay for the sins of the world. This explains why
I'm always confused when I read about times when Jesus caused
his parents, especially his mother, to worry. Does this mean
that Jesus—the perfect son of God—sinned?

The second chapter of Luke, verses 41–52, contains a story
that might make you think Jesus did just that. This passage
tells about a time when Jesus went to Jerusalem with his parents. Apparently, however, he decided to stay in the city when
his parents headed home. The Bible makes it clear that Mary
and Joseph were unaware of his decision. This seems to show
that Jesus, the Savior of the world, the one kid who always did
the right thing, Jesus . . . dumped his parents!

If your twelve-year-old boy pulled a stunt like this, would
you not call it a sin? Let's say you take a family trip to Disney
World, and your oldest son decides, completely on his own,

that he's just not ready to leave when you do. It's been a long, tiring day, and you gather the family to begin your trip home. You pull out of the parking lot, thinking your son is in the back of the van. A few hours down the road, you suddenly realize that you haven't seen or heard him for a long time. All at once, it hits you, and you turn around, questioning, "Where's your brother? Have you seen your brother? When was the last time you saw your brother? Where can he be?"

Imagine the anger, fear, and frustration you would feel. *Can you believe that boy? What do you suppose he was thinking? After all, he's only twelve years old!* No doubt, all these thoughts run through your brain—and possibly even leave your mouth—as you turn the van around and head back down the highway toward the park.

In her own time, Mary experienced something very close to this Disney World scenario. The Bible says that she and Joseph had traveled a day's journey from Jerusalem when she first noticed Jesus' absence. Most likely, they walked in a long caravan, men separate from women, so it's very possible that Mary and Joseph eventually turned to each other and said what exasperated parents say today: "I thought *you* had him."

Mothers seem to have a sixth sense where their children are concerned, so I'm sure Mary was the first to notice that Jesus was not along for the ride—er, walk. Imagine: she begins to ask her relatives and acquaintances, "Where's Jesus? Have you seen Jesus? Have you seen him?"

"No."

"No."

"No, I haven't seen him." Imagine her mounting concern and fear as she hears these answers repeated. She goes to Joseph, heartbroken and sobbing. The two find themselves an entire day away from the city where their son is lost—and of course, they can't even begin their search until they return to Jerusalem. Mary has to spend the whole night praying and worrying as she waits to leave early in the morning. Can you imagine her prayer? "Dear God, I've lost him. I've lost the Savior of the world."

"You did WHAT? WHAT? You lost my only begotten son?"

"Wait, Lord, I promise—I'm going back to look for him as soon as it gets light outside!"

The next morning, Mary and Joseph head back to Jerusalem. Once they arrive, Mary is sure every child who passes by must be her missing son. "There he is!" "No, there he is—!" Again and again, she is disappointed when the child moves or turns slightly and she realizes the truth—not one of them is Jesus, after all. Joseph, on the other hand, has to be thinking exactly what I would be thinking after backtracking all that way with a worried, frightened wife at my side: *When I get my hands on that boy, he won't be able to sit down for a week*!

LOST AND FOUND

Luke's account goes on to tell us that Mary and Joseph *do* find Jesus—not one, not two, but *three* entire days later, sitting in the temple, listening to the teachers and asking them questions. Scripture even tells us that everyone who heard him was "astonished at his understanding and his answers" (Luke 2:47 NKJV).

His parents are astonished too—but their astonishment takes a slightly different form. As soon as Mary sees Jesus, she rips into him lovingly, as only an angry mother can: "Son, how could you treat us this way? *Oy, vey!*"

We really can't blame her. If you were in this situation, how would you respond? Mary simply unleashes on Jesus all her pent-up anger and worry from a long day of travel and three longer days of scouring the city.

Let's review. Mary and Joseph have just spent three days looking for their twelve-year-old son, who didn't tell them in the first place that he was going to be staying behind in Jerusalem. My mom and dad would have considered that a major sin. Then Jesus has the nerve to ask, "Why were you looking for me?" In today's language, we could translate that using just one word: "Duh!"

I said something like that to my dad once . . . but only once.

THE REST OF THE STORY

Let's stop right here. If Jesus was perfect, and if Jesus never sinned, then how was his behavior *not* sinful? When I ask this question, people offer all sorts of different explanations. Some tell me that Mary and Joseph were bad parents. Obviously, they should have been more on top of things and known where he was at all times.

I have a problem with that idea. After all, Mary and Joseph were good enough parents that God entrusted them with his own Son! You can't get much better than that. As a matter of fact, you're a much better parent than you think you are, too—even if you've had a child get away from you in the store, the way my Caleb did once.

It only took a moment, but I turned around and . . . he wasn't there. I began to race through the aisles, my heart pumping and my eyes sweeping frantically from side to side as I called out, "Caleb! Caleb!" Mary and Joseph were *not* bad parents. Neither am I. Neither are you.

Perhaps you've already guessed what I believe is the rest of the story—the real truth behind this passage. The reason that Jesus was not sinning when he stayed behind in Jerusalem was that he had already experienced something that made him very different from today's McDonald's Kids. Jesus had experienced a rite of passage. He had gone through his Bar Mitzvah and assumed his place as a man.

For Adults Only

In the Jewish culture of Jesus' day, every adult had to go to Jerusalem once a year, so at age twelve, Jesus traveled there— as an adult. By making this trip, he was taking on an adult responsibility, so he was also taking on adult consequences for the decisions he made.

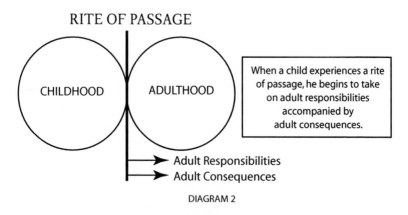

RITE OF PASSAGE

CHILDHOOD   ADULTHOOD

When a child experiences a rite of passage, he begins to take on adult responsibilities accompanied by adult consequences.

Adult Responsibilities
Adult Consequences

DIAGRAM 2

As an adult, I travel quite often. Is it inappropriate or unusual for me to make a decision to stay an extra day or two in a city before going on to my next destination? Of course not! I may have business I need to finish. Special circumstances may arise that require an adjustment in my schedule. I'm an adult. I can change my plans, and I have to deal with the adult consequences of those plans. I may have to rent a car for another day or two. I will have to arrange for a place to stay for the extra nights I'll be in that area. And of course, I have to make arrangements to eat . . . you can be sure I don't forget that adjustment.

Jesus' decision to stay behind in Jerusalem was also an adult decision. Where did he sleep? I've been to Jerusalem, and they don't have a Motel 6 there. Maybe he stayed in the "Passover Palace"—you know, the one with the popular slogan, "Moses Slept Here." What did Jesus eat during those extra days when his parents weren't there to provide his food? I don't know if McDavid's was there at that time or not, but I do know that, as an adult, Jesus had to take care of his own meals.

Look again at the Scripture passage. Jesus had taken on adult responsibilities: he was listening, asking questions, and amazing the teachers. Can you imagine today's average twelve-year-old dialoguing with the "lawyers of the lawyers" as Jesus did? Jesus had moved into his adult life because he had experienced a rite of passage. He was a capable, responsible, self-reliant young man because his culture and his family had built this specific event into his life.

Jesus did *not* sin. All parents have to adjust when their kids begin to grow up. Mary and Joseph were no exception—and yet, their son did not sin against them. He had completed his passage into adulthood by taking on adult responsibilities and adult consequences, even in the way he returned home with his parents and willingly submitted himself to them as his *authority*. Maybe that's why Mary "treasured all these things in her heart" (v. 51) as her son "grew in favor with God and man" (v. 52). Like all mothers, she had to adjust to the fact that her little boy was now . . . a man.

‣ AUTHORITY: A designated person or persons to whom an individual voluntarily submits his will.

ADOLESCENCE: A NEW INVENTION

When our society completed the agricultural-to-industrial shift in the early 1950s, we also began to delay the time when our children took on adult responsibilities, such as running a business or working in a factory. At the same time, we didn't want our adult-sized children sitting around building with blocks or playing with puzzles, so we invented a new concept. Our culture began to call this in-between time *adolescence*. The definition itself means that adolescents have left their childhood behind but have not yet embraced their adulthood. In effect, they are caught between two worlds. Psychologist Ronald Koteskey uses the following diagram to explain the problem:

SHIFT IN PARENTING MODEL

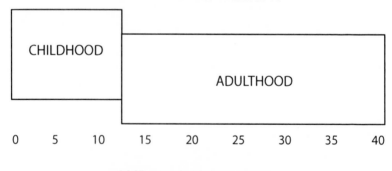

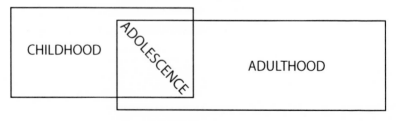

DIAGRAM 3 [1]

Koteskey notes that our culture has *created* or *invented* this concept of adolescence. In many other cultures, and in ours before it shifted so dramatically, people go directly from childhood to adulthood without passing through this confusing time. The top section of Koteskey's diagram shows a culture that has periods of childhood and adulthood, but no adolescence. He explains:

As you see in the second part of [diagram 3], today we have a period during which childhood and adulthood overlap. This invention of adolescence has created problems primarily in the areas of identity, sexuality, work, and school. As long as we have adolescence, we will face these problems.[2]

THE INVENTION OF ADOLESCENCE

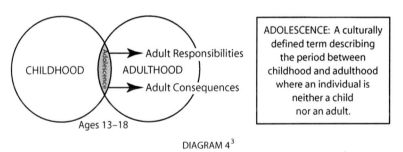

DIAGRAM 4[3]

New Testament scholar and seminary professor Dr. David Alan Black explains the confusion of the false concept of adolescence:

Clearly, the invention of adolescence has altered the process of growing up in America. When school, church, and family treat sixteen-year-olds like young children, teenagers act in ways that justify that treatment. Little wonder today's young people are suffering from role confusion. They don't know who they are, where they came from, or where they are headed. They are at the starting gate of life with no place to go.[4]

PENDULUM EFFECT

Our culture's invention of adolescence set a pendulum in motion. That pendulum started at the point where even very young teens had the skills and abilities to live as mature, responsible adults. Because of the agricultural-industrial cultural shift, the point where young people achieve true maturity has caused the pendulum to swing father and farther away from its starting point. That's confusing and scary for the young people caught in the trap of adolescence as well as for their families.

However, while the *pendulum of adult responsibility* is swinging farther and farther away from birth, another pendulum has begun a gradual swing completely in the opposite direction. This is the *pendulum of physical maturity*—the point at which an individual becomes capable of biological reproduction. In fact, research shows that kids today are experiencing puberty—the point of physical maturity—at a much younger age than they did a century or two ago.

> Before 1850, the average woman first menstruated at about sixteen years of age . . . Not a single one of the sixty-five studies done before 1880 found an average age below fourteen and a half. Many were seventeen or more. By 1950 however, the average was down to about twelve and a half or thirteen.
>
> Puberty in men is not as obvious and has not been studied as much. However, when Bach was choirmaster at St. Thomas Church in Leipzig more than two hundred

years ago, boys often sang soprano until they were seventeen. . . . In 1744, Bach had ten altos [those whose voices were changing], the youngest was fifteen and the oldest nineteen. Men's voices changed at about seventeen years of age then, but at about thirteen or fourteen now. . . . This change takes place at about the age of puberty.

All of this means that people today experience puberty about three or four years earlier than they did only a century or two ago.[5]

As our culture has pushed the pendulum of adult responsibility farther and farther away from childhood—some now say as late as twenty-six years of age—the pendulum of physical maturity swings closer and closer to the time of birth.

Think about it. Experiencing just one of these swinging pendulums would create confusion. Having them *both* swinging in opposite directions—working simultaneously against one another—wreaks havoc for the young person, for his or her family, and for our society. This has caused the chaos that adolescents face today. The lack of a rite of passage has created a new creature, one that our world has never seen before.

Who is this strange being? He has every physical attribute of a man, but he lacks the skills and abilities to survive on his own—and, in all likelihood, he won't acquire those qualities for a long time. This previously unknown creature is someone we call the adolescent. He looks like a man but acts like a child. He is scary . . . very scary! Again, Koteskey explains it well:

Adolescence has been created and handed to us. Like Shelley's Dr. Frankenstein, our culture has created a monster and is having trouble controlling it. Some people call adolescence "a period of temporary insanity between childhood and adulthood." They are right, but it is not the teenager that is insane. It is our culture. Our crazy culture invented adolescence . . . and now we do not know what to do with it.[6]

> ⤙ ADOLESCENCE: A culturally defined term describing the period between childhood and adulthood when an individual is neither a child nor an adult.
> ⤙ PENDULUM OF ADULT RESPONSIBILITY: The point at which an individual assumes adult responsibilities (the obligations of an individual for his own life and for others over whom he has authority).
> ⤙ PENDULUM OF PHYSICAL MATURITY: The point at which an individual becomes capable of biological reproduction.

WHEN DOES ADULTHOOD BEGIN?

From the beginning of time, societies all over the world have known exactly when a child became an adult. Over the past few years, however, since our own culture does not provide children with a definite rite of passage, the dividing line doesn't seem nearly as clear.

The number one thing that every child wants to know is, "When do I become an adult?" In our culture, you're able to get a driver's license at age sixteen, so *that* must be when you become an adult. But wait . . . you can't vote until you're eighteen, so *that* must be when you become an adult. But wait . . . you can't drink alcohol until you're twenty-one, so *that* must be when you become an adult. But wait . . . you can't rent a car until you're twenty-five, so *that* must be when you become an adult . . .

Do you get the picture? Instead of drawing a clear-cut line between childhood and adulthood via a rite of passage, our culture sends mixed messages. Most adolescents tell me that half of the world tells them to get lost, and the other half tells them to find themselves!

THE EXTENSION OF ADOLESCENCE

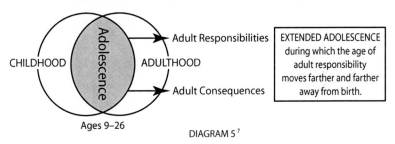

CHILDHOOD — Adolescence — ADULTHOOD → Adult Responsibilities → Adult Consequences

EXTENDED ADOLESCENCE during which the age of adult responsibility moves farther and farther away from birth.

Ages 9–26

DIAGRAM 5 [7]

In the midst of this confusion, you'll be glad to know that I have finally found an organization that will provide a definite rite of passage for your children. You can go to one of their locations anywhere in the country, and each one provides exactly the same experience. I'll spell out the name of this unique spot: D-e-n-n-y's. Yes, Denny's Restaurant will gladly provide your child with the rite of passage that kids are missing today.

Just try it. Take your child to Denny's when he has just turned thirteen years old, and ask for the "adolescent" menu. You may get a laugh—or you may get a hostess who thinks you're crazy. The staff at Denny's will quickly let you know that they do *not* have an adolescent menu. They have one menu for children twelve and under. When you order from this menu, you get the box of crayons, macaroni and cheese, chicken nuggets, and kiddie cups.

Once you pass twelve years of age, Denny's immediately considers you an adult. All of a sudden, they take away the children's menu. You can try taking a napkin and drawing a diagram to show them the gray area of adolescence, but it won't work. They *won't* pull out an adolescent menu, and they *will* expect you to pay for your meal. Denny's is one place in America that has no adolescence. (Note: Denny's continues to provide children with a rite of passage—but today, they will get to experience it at an even younger age. After writing this book, I learned that the kids' menu at Denny's now applies only to children ten and under.)

Movie theaters are another place with a no-adolescence philosophy. Kids pay one expensive price; and adults pay another, even more expensive price. I've noticed the same thing about Tylenol. Do you remember what it says on the back of the Tylenol bottle? Children twelve and under, take one tablet; ages twelve and over, two tablets. Where is the adolescent dosage?

You know, that question always made sense until the manufacturer came out with Tylenol Junior. In case you haven't figured it out, that's how the smart people at Tylenol now get you to buy more of their product. You only need one adult Tylenol—but you have to buy two of the Junior brand to get the same amount of medicine. Apparently, their marketing experts figured out that adolescence isn't such a bad thing, after all.

OH, GROW UP!: FALSE RITES OF PASSAGE

I've figured out something myself—and I bet you've noticed it too. Every child is born with the God-given desire to grow up. Little girls love to wear mommy's dress, put on mommy's hat, and tromp around in high heels. Long before they're tall enough to reach the lawnmower handles, little boys want to help their dads cut the grass. God has placed within each of us the desire to grow up. However, our society does not provide a definite way for children to do that. Here's an example of the way this shows in the life of Little Johnny, who may live next door . . . or right there in your own home.

Little Johnny is in third grade. Since our culture doesn't give him a way to leave his childhood behind, he begins carrying an invisible basket everywhere he goes—his way of keeping track of the things he does that others in his world might consider an adult activity. Little Johnny thinks, *If I collect enough adult activities in my basket, someone will pronounce me an adult. I don't know the magic number, so I'm not sure how many adult activities I need . . . but I'm going to keep collecting them.*

Since no one tells Little Johnny, *"This is how you become an adult,"* he goes to school one day and says a *very* bad word. When his teacher questions him, he tells her, "I heard it from my dad." In Little Johnny's world, grown-ups use this kind of language, and he is trying desperately to prove to his peers that he is growing up. He has chosen one of the first and most common activities that kids use as a *false rite of passage,* an artificial means of marking the line between childhood and adulthood. Our kids create these counterfeit passages into adult life because we don't provide them with the real thing.

- ⟜ ADULT ACTIVITIES: Actions that identify an individual as an adult according to personal or cultural norms.
- ⟜ FALSE RITE OF PASSAGE: An artificial means of marking the line between childhood and adulthood.

Since Little Johnny needs to figure out even more ways of becoming an adult, he puts rebellion into his basket. Next, he adds smoking—right alongside the rebellion. Surely you've seen Little Johnny. He's the guy leaning against the wall in the yard of the middle school, puffing away on his cigarette. Little Johnny is in seventh grade, six feet tall and eighty pounds. His narrowed eyes say it all: "Look at me; I'm a man." His girlfriend is standing there smoking, too. You recognize her. She's the one with her bra on backward—it fits better that way.

Both Little Johnny and his girlfriend are trying desperately to grow up. Since our culture doesn't give them a way to accomplish that by providing a rite of passage, they create their own ways to reach adulthood. One reason that alcohol use has become so widespread among today's teens is that high school students think that drinking (another false rite of passage) proves they're more grown up than they were in junior high. After all, I can't possibly live with the mind-set that says I'm still a child. If I'm able to drink, I must be grown up.

In some places in Panama, you receive a henna tattoo to show your adult connection to the tribe. How do you become part of the adult tribe in America? The current generation has chosen two particular activities as its own rites of passage: tattooing and body piercing. After all, when you're a child, you can't even use a magic marker to write on your hand without getting in trouble! Today's generation believes that tattoos and piercings tell others, "I have the ability to make adult decisions for my life."

When I was growing up, young women had to wait until their sixteenth birthday to get their ears pierced, and until about that same age to wear hose. Today, many little girls wear pantyhose and have their ears pierced even before they go to kindergarten. Things that used to be rites of passage—things you had to wait for, things that we formerly considered as marks of closing down childhood—have now become a normal part of life, even for very young children. When do we grow up? Our culture doesn't know . . . and it's definitely not telling our kids.

Tired Out

For seven years, I served as a chaplain with the Tulsa Police Department. One of my responsibilities was to handle the suicide calls for a lower-income area of town. This included notifying the families when a death had occurred. I also worked with gangs. Tulsa, somewhat surprisingly, has a tremendous amount of gang activity, including five times the national average of gang fights every year. As I watched these gangs, I began to learn about why these close-knit, often violent groups formed.

You don't just *join* a gang—you have to pass a test of some kind that serves as your initiation. In this way, gangs meet two very basic needs in each child's life: a rite of passage and a meaningful role. Our culture's confused, disconnected young people embrace gang membership in increasing numbers because we no longer provide these basic requirements.

Again . . . I should know. As a five-year-old, when my family moved away from the country, I experienced a tentative introduction to gang life on the inner city streets of Kansas City, Missouri. My family relocated to a downtown area so that my dad could take a better job. In the process, he unwittingly moved his wife and sons into a rough neighborhood.

In order to find acceptance with the kids in my brand-new setting, I decided to join a gang. The other members told me that if I could slash forty tires, I would belong. They quickly taught me a crucial skill: how to take a razor blade and cut the stem from a tire. Somehow, I slipped out of the house after dark one night and got busy slashing away at my forty-tire requirement—all on our side of the street. I wasn't allowed to cross to the other side; after all, I was only five years old.

The next day, the police came looking for me. I'm not sure how they found out, but I think it had something to do with the fact that my dad's car was the only one on our block whose tires remained intact. I hated to think what might happen if Dad found out that I had so much as touched his car.

Naturally, when the police questioned me, I did what any smart kid would do: I denied everything. Unfortunately, my three-year-old brother, who greatly admired my tire-slashing skills, was more than ready to brag on me to the officers. My life of crime ended very abruptly—and, by the way, that tattle-tale brother is now Missouri's lead state patrolman, in charge of security for the governor himself.

Even as a five-year-old in a bad neighborhood, I wanted to belong. I wanted to be considered grown up. I wanted a rite of passage. Kids today seem to need it even more than I did. That's why the length of the period that our culture calls *adolescence* continues to increase.

I know what those twenty- and thirty-something adolescents are doing—they're out collecting adult activities to fill their baskets. They haven't become the capable, responsible, self-reliant adults that the young people of previous generations became at much earlier ages. Today's young people are largely incapable, irresponsible, and, especially, confused.

HELICOPTER PARENTS

Because our children are so confused about who they are and what they can do, parents have now decided that they must follow their kids nearly everywhere they go. Since the kids haven't taken on adult responsibilities—they can't live, act, or communicate as adults—mom and dad have to travel alongside to help take care of them.

Today's schoolteachers, Little League coaches, and even university officials regularly confront overinvolved parents who believe they need to take up the slack for their irresponsible kids. Psychologist Pamela Paul uses a special term, *helicopter parents*, to refer to these too-close-for-comfort moms and dads:

> Not surprisingly, parental involvement in kids' lives has pushed its way onto campuses, where "helicopter parents" hover, trying to help their kids through college financially, emotionally, and even academically. Parents have been known to intervene in roommate disputes following an emotional e-mail plea from a child, or call a professor to question a grade. In response, universities are scheduling special parent orientation events, hiring parental "liaisons" to handle questions and demands, and firing off terse-but-diplomatic guidelines.
>
> The days when parents simply dropped their kids off and waved goodbye are as antiquated as the college mixer.[8]

Paul notes that even the Harvard College *Handbook for Parents* contains messages aimed at overly involved parents. These warnings intentionally place the responsibility for academic life back upon the student and encourage interfering parents to back off and away . . . now.[9]

Our culture contains plenty of these helicopter parents. The problem has even reached the workplace. "Managers [of various companies] are getting phone calls from parents asking them to hire their twenty-something kids. Candidates are stalling on job offers to consult with their parents. Parents are calling hiring managers to protest pay packages and try to renegotiate, employers say."[10]

Remember the Waltons? John and Olivia never followed

their son around solving his problems or fighting his battles. If John-Boy had a struggle of some kind, he took care of it him-self—like the man his parents knew he was. Yes, he consulted his family—especially his grandpa—but ultimately, the adult responsibilities and adult consequences of his actions belonged only to him. The helicopter parent, like the adolescent, is a cultural creation—one that will continue to increase in number if we don't do something to stop the growing trend of irresponsible, incapable, immature young adults.

> ✦ HELICOPTER PARENTS: Moms and dads who hover above their children because they don't think the kids are capable of handling things on their own.
>
> ✦ BOOMERANG GENERATION (also "Boomerangs"): Young adults who refuse to be self-reliant and keep returning to their authority for the basic needs of life.
>
> ✦ B2BS OR BACK-TO-BEDROOM KIDS: Jobless or under-employed Boomerangs who have returned to their parents' homes to live.

THE BOOMERANG GENERATION

This trend of irresponsibility is so well-known that we have even coined a new term for its subculture—the *Boomerang Generation*. These young adults refuse to be self-reliant and keep returning to their authority for the basic needs of life. Today, more and more families have become part of this trend. One mother of three adult daughters said:

> We never went back and lived with our parents, but my daughter came back to live with us for a year to save money. It's like a revolving door. The kids go out

for a while, and if they're not immediately successful, or they need a change, or they need time to accumulate funds to take their next step, they move home in between. I have a lot of friends whose children have moved back home, married, with or without children, in between jobs. Some can't seem to move on with their lives.[11]

In fact, a 2003 study by the National Opinion Research Center showed that most Americans don't consider a person an adult until age twenty-six or until he or she has finished school, works full time, and has begun to raise a family.

Futurist Faith Popcorn has created another new term, *B2Bs* or *Back-to-Bedroom Kids*. This trend continues to increase, as tracked by the 2000 census, which showed four million people between the ages of twenty-five and thirty-four who lived with their parents. In a 2003 Monster/JobTrak.com poll, 61 percent of college seniors said they expected to move back home after graduation.[12] A *Time* magazine article also examines this trend.

[These B2Bs] aren't lazy, the argument goes, they're reaping the fruit of decades of American affluence and social liberation. This new period is a chance for young people to savor the pleasures of irresponsibility, search their souls and choose their life paths. . . . Researchers fear that whatever cultural machinery used to turn kids into grownups has broken down, that society no longer provides young people with the moral backbone and the financial wherewithal to take their rightful places in the adult world. Could growing up be harder than it used to be?[13]

I have to say it, mom and dad. The *last* thing I want is my kids moving back home. You mean I have to take care of them when they're young, pay their college expenses, and then take care of them after college too? No, thanks!

When we don't provide our kids with a rite of passage, they end up like the B2Bs: confused. When we look back at the life of Jesus, we realize that he was never a teenager in the modern sense. He never had to go through the miserable confusion of adolescence or the extended irresponsibility of B2Bs—and your kids can avoid this too. Through *Rite of Passage Parenting*, I want to help you provide a way for your child to make the transition from childhood to capable, responsible, adulthood. Let's look at how we can help equip your kids . . . for life.

⤳ Rite of Passage Parenting Summary ⤳

Jesus experienced a clear rite of passage through the Jewish custom of Bar Mitzvah. He demonstrated this when he went to the temple in Jerusalem at age twelve, taking on adult responsibilities and adult consequences.

Our culture has invented the concept of adolescence, and we have also begun to increase the age of expected adult responsibility while the age of physical maturity continues to drop. Since our society is confused about when adulthood begins, many young people take on false rites of passage in order to prove to the world that they are grown up. Others extend their childhood by boomeranging back to their childhood bedrooms. Parents support this trend by becoming hovering helicopter parents who can't seem to let their children go. At the same time, we tell our kids, "Why can't you just grow up?"

༄

CHAPTER THREE

ESSENTIAL EXPERIENCE #1:
MARK THEIR MATURITY
THROUGH A RITE OF PASSAGE

We can help provide closure to our kids' childhood by providing avenues for them to mark their maturity through a rite of passage.

Let's go back to John-Boy Walton, our favorite young man from the Blue Ridge Mountains. Once again, think about John-Boy—not as we would have seen him during the Depression Era but as we might see him today.

Our modern John-Boy comes sauntering out to meet his grandfather. The first thing we notice is that his faded, torn blue jeans are at least three sizes too big. The waistband rides low on his hips, exposing polka-dotted boxer shorts hiked up so far that they appear to cover his belly button. His brightly colored shirt, in a size designed to fit John Wayne better than John-Boy, contrasts with the paisley bandanna wrapped too tightly around his head and the sparkling chains that dangle from his neck.

John-Boy carelessly shuffles up to Grandpa, leaning slightly to one side. He holds his arms tightly against his chest, his hands dangle limply, and both his shoelaces are untied. Grandpa doesn't know whether to laugh aloud at this unusual creature or get out his gun and put it out of its misery.

Suddenly, the bejeweled John-Boy speaks. "Yo, Pops! 'Sup? Like the new bling-bling? 'S phat! I wuz jes', like, chillin' with my homies—a'ight?"

This imaginary picture makes us laugh because we know that the real John-Boy never dreamed of dressing, speaking, or acting this way. The Walton's Mountain John-Boy wore adult clothing, used adult speech, and practiced adult behavior because he lived as an adult. The agricultural society in which he lived provided him with an *informal* rite of passage.

John-Boy's society—and certainly his family—had closed down his childhood, and he had the unwritten expectation (an informal rite of passage) that he was now to live and act as an adult. As an adult, he would certainly never have addressed his grandfather in the way described above . . . any more than Grandpa Walton would have told him to "get jiggy widdit." John-Boy moved forward into full adult responsibility at an age where most of today's young people are generally considered "just kids" who can't be held responsible for anything.

CALEB AND THE FREE APARTMENT GUIDES

Although our culture tells us we can't expect young people to behave responsibly, God has placed within every child the desire to do grown-up things. My son Caleb was no exception. During our sons' early years, our family lived in a suburban neighborhood. Conveniently, our house happened to be just a few blocks from a small grocery store. Because we lived so close to this market, our boys were some of its best customers.

One day when Caleb was about four years old, he came home with a whole stack of free apartment guides—you know, the kind you see near the checkout lanes at almost every super-market. "What are you going to do with those, Caleb?" I asked, curious about his heavy burden.

"I'm gonna sell 'em."

I laughed at his innocent air. Being the wise dad that I am, I recognized this as the time for one of those important father-son chats—a few precious moments in which I could impart valuable wisdom to my boy. First, I knew that I needed to explain the word *free* emblazoned on the cover of each guide. "You see, son, if something's *free*, that means anyone can have one."

"But, Dad—," Caleb managed.

I continued, sure that he would soon see the error of his ways. "Caleb, you can't sell something that's free. The store gives these books away."

"But, Dad—," he tried again.

"And Caleb," I was really warming up now. "These are *apartment* guides. Son, we live in a *residential* neighborhood. That means families live in their own homes."

"But, Dad—" There was the little voice again.

Now I was getting frustrated. "Caleb, no one in a residential neighborhood even *needs* an apartment guide! And you can't sell something that's free!"

"But, Dad—" All thoughts of educating my son had now departed.

"Caleb Henry! You take those apartment guides back to the store right now, and put them all on the rack where you got them! Do you understand me?"

His blue eyes looked a bit wistful as he made one final plea, "But, Dad—"

I swallowed two or three times as I fought for composure. "Caleb, what is it?"

"Dad—this is my second load." As he spoke, my son reached

his grimy fingers deep into the pocket of his blue jeans and pulled out, not one or two, but a whole handful of quarters.

I was the one who received an education that day. Who knew that you could make money selling free apartment guides? Of course—Caleb did, even at four years old. Making money is an adult responsibility, something grownups generally accomplish by having a job. Caleb wanted to do something to show that he was growing up, and his self-appointed job of selling free apartment guides met that need perfectly . . . even in a residential neighborhood.

PREPARATION, EVENT, AND CELEBRATION

What can you do to provide closure for your kids' childhood, equipping them for life by helping them move into responsible adulthood? You already know the answer: you provide a rite of passage, a definite step between the two realms. However, you don't just wake up your child one day with the words, "The time is here. Today . . . you are an adult!"

In the Jewish culture, children hear about their upcoming rites of passage as soon as they are born. From their earliest days, their parents consciously and deliberately cast into them a vision for adulthood. They tell their children again and again that a day will come when they will lead in temple worship, share a memorized portion of the Torah, and begin to accept adult responsibilities. The Mitzvah ceremony is an event in which the child demonstrates adult skills. However, it is also a celebration of the preparation that has brought the child to this point.

The overall definition for rite of passage includes all three components: preparation, event, and celebration. *Rite of Passage Parenting* teaches you how to use these elements, along with those discussed in the three remaining sections of the book, to incorporate back into your kids' lives the four essential experiences that our culture lost when it shifted.

- **INFORMAL RITE OF PASSAGE:** A distinction between childhood and adulthood marked by adult responsibilities and adult consequences rather than formal recognition through an event and/or celebration.
- **RITE OF PASSAGE:** A clearly defined line that distinguishes childhood from adulthood. Includes the following components.
- **RITE OF PASSAGE PREPARATION:** A series of incremental tasks designed to build adult responsibilities into an individual's life, preparing him for the transition from childhood to responsible adulthood.
- **RITE OF PASSAGE EVENT:** A step that moves an individual quickly and definitely from childhood to responsible adulthood.
- **RITE OF PASSAGE CELEBRATION:** A formal recognition by family and friends that acknowledges the crossing over of the line between childhood and adulthood.
- **EMERGING ADULTHOOD:** State in which young people have experienced a rite of passage and gradually assume full adult responsibilities and adult consequences.

HOME ALONE

One of the things we accomplish through Awe Star Ministries, the organization I founded, is teaching students how to live in our multicultural world. We no longer have the privilege of isolating ourselves in a single culture. Back when I was growing up in rural Missouri, I had no exposure to international foods or travel. Today, people have many choices of multicultural restaurants, and their jobs often take them into different parts of the world. In fact, companies are looking for employees with international mind-sets. Awe Star Ministries helps provide young people with the skills to adapt to a global world.

During the writing of this book, I led a group of Awe Star students to experience the culture of the Embera Puru. This people group, with whom our ministry has a strong relationship, originates in the jungles of Panama near the Colombian border. While living among the Embera Puru, I follow Paul's example and "become all things to all men" (1 Cor. 9:22 NKJV). I take on tribal tattoos, assume adult responsibilities as a member of the tribe, and observe their culture from this inside vantage point.

One day during one of my visits with the Embera Puru, their chief pointed to his twelve-year-old sister-in-law and told me she would be getting married next year. Curious, I asked about the wedding ceremony. He told me that his people do not have one. What they have instead is a well-defined rite of passage.

In the Embera Puru culture, at around twelve to fourteen years of age, a young man and a young woman build a house together. They work side by side every day, making their house from the wood, vines, and grasses they find in the jungle. During the construction period, they return separately to their parents' homes every night. When the house is finished, they move into it . . . together.

Once the two young people have accomplished the adult task of house building, the tribe views them as married and, just as importantly, considers them adults. In this way, house building serves as the Embera Puru tribe's rite of passage event.

Deep in the jungles of Panama, no one wonders whether these two young people will be able to traverse their rite of passage event. ("Do you think they can do it? Will they be able to build that house?" "Oh, I hope so! Maybe we oughtta go help them!") Their culture has prepared the couple from childhood for this defining moment. Small children learn to weave the vines that will form the roof for their house. They carry and practice carving the wood that will become stilts to support its structure. Mastering each of these tasks—designed to build adult responsibilities into their lives, preparing them for the transition from childhood to responsible adulthood— ensures that each of them is ready for a rite of passage event.

EMBERA PURU RITE OF PASSAGE

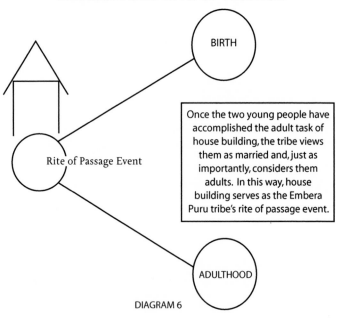

BIRTH

Rite of Passage Event

Once the two young people have accomplished the adult task of house building, the tribe views them as married and, just as importantly, considers them adults. In this way, house building serves as the Embera Puru tribe's rite of passage event.

ADULTHOOD

DIAGRAM 6

At the Crossroads

Scripture teaches us to "Stand by the ways and see and ask for the ancient paths, where the good way is, and walk in it; And you will find rest for your souls" (Jer. 6:16 NASB).

As parents, many of us find ourselves standing at a crossroads in our relationships with our kids. We just don't know what to do. In these situations, we may feel like McDavid's parents trying to work with McDonald's Kids. After all, we were raised to respect our elders, to take responsibility for our actions, and to respond with adult speech and conduct. Somehow, however, the culture has shifted and our kids have missed out. We're at the crossroads.

On the other hand, some of us were raised as McDonald's Kids ourselves. Our parents did not build the ancient paths of adult responsibilities and skills for living into our lives. As a result, we have no idea how to build these important experiences into the lives of our children. We're at the crossroads too.

When you're at the crossroads, you have to make a decision: walk, or don't walk. Are you going to follow the ancient paths, the good way that we know produces responsible, capable children, or are you going to continue walking down the paths our culture has built?

Both paths have predictable results. We know that raising children the way our culture prescribes does not produce responsible, self-reliant adults. Those paths end in rebellious, back-talking kids who can't take care of themselves. Since you're at the crossroads, it's not too late for you to change the way you walk—the way you choose to parent your child. Whether your child is sixteen, seventeen, even thirty years of age . . . it's not too late.

I can help you fix it by teaching you Rite of Passage Parenting. We've been walking down the wrong path, and we don't want to go that way anymore. Look to the ancient path, and learn. Walk, or don't walk—it's your choice.

LUNAR SLINGSHOT

As a youth minister, still frustrated because the students I worked with never seemed to reach responsible, capable adulthood, I finally began to study the *tried and true road* that the Bible sets forth. I knew there would come a point when we had to recast a student's life away from childhood and toward an adult orientation. One day I was talking to my friend Tom, an engineer who designs boosters for the space shuttle program, about this idea. He began to tell me about something that he considers a very basic concept.

Tom explained that the rocket engines used to launch the satellites and space shuttles don't carry nearly enough power to move these heavy spacecraft from one planet to another. In order to acquire a needed boost, they take advantage of an amazing effect that scientists call the *lunar slingshot*. This scientific phenomenon, also called a *gravity assist*, uses the gravitational pull of the moon to accelerate a spacecraft's momentum and to recast its trajectory in a new direction. Its effectiveness has made it a standard part of modern space flight.

Let's say a probe is leaving Earth, heading toward Mars for an expedition. First, the aeronautical experts aim their spacecraft at the moon. As it leaves Earth's gravity, it begins to enter the sun's gravitational pull. Eventually, however, the gravitational pull of the moon begins to draw the craft toward the lunar surface with increasing speed.

At that precise moment, scientists utilize the moon's gravity as a lunar slingshot, changing the direction of the probe and shooting it off in an entirely new direction—in this case, toward Mars—at a faster speed. This specific part of the probe's trajectory, called the *breaking point,* occurs when scientists use the combined acceleration and new gravitational pull of a spacecraft to reset its course. Without this gravity assist, the spacecraft would not have enough momentum to reach its ultimate destination.

The first spacecraft to experience a gravity assist was NASA's Pioneer 10. In December 1973, it approached a rendezvous with Jupiter, the largest planet in the Solar System, traveling at 9.8 kilometers per second. Following its passage through Jupiter's gravitational field, it sped off into deep space at 22.4 kilometers a second— like when you let go of a spinning merry-go-round and fly off in one direction. This kind of acceleration is also called the *slingshot effect.*[1]

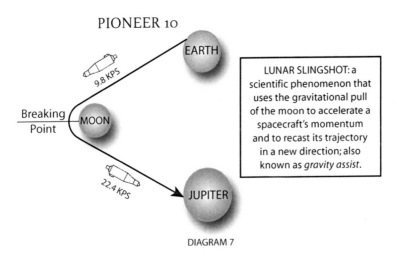

PIONEER 10

EARTH

9.8 KPS

Breaking Point

MOON

LUNAR SLINGSHOT: a scientific phenomenon that uses the gravitational pull of the moon to accelerate a spacecraft's momentum and to recast its trajectory in a new direction; also known as *gravity assist.*

22.4 KPS

JUPITER

DIAGRAM 7

Parenting *Is* Rocket Science

Keeping the lunar slingshot in mind, if someone tells you that parenting isn't rocket science ... he or she is wrong. Let's use this model to help us understand this idea of recasting our kids' lives from the path of childhood into the path of responsible adult living.

Mom and dad, when your child is born, she needs to stay close to you. She depends on you to provide everything she needs: food, shelter, and clean diapers—not to mention a crib model iPod. If this child is going to become a capable, responsible, self-reliant adult, she has a long way to go. She needs rite of passage preparation so she can gradually take on more and more adult responsibilities. Like Pioneer 10 headed toward Jupiter, a moment comes when she accelerates enough to reach a breaking point, when she leaves your direct influence. At that point she can head off in a brand-new direction with even more momentum and a fresh focus. In other words, she is now ready for a rite of passage event.

> ⚬ BREAKING POINT: The point at which scientists use the combined acceleration and new gravitational pull of a spacecraft to reset its course.

Many cultures have a defining experience that determines the rite of passage event. For the Embera Puru people, it's house building. In some areas of the Spanish-speaking world, it's the *quinceañera*, the elaborate celebration traditionally held when a young woman turns fifteen. For the Jewish people, it's the Bar or Bat Mitzvah.

After the Mitzvah ceremony, Jewish young people are ready to show the world that they can do adult things. Are they fully adult just because they have gone through the ceremony? Of course not. Though these young people have experienced a rite of passage, they will gradually assume full adult responsibilities and consequences. They are what I prefer to call *emerging adults*.

The rite of passage event is the dividing line that changes the trajectory of the child's life, shooting it along a new course and causing it to gain even more momentum toward capable, responsible, self-reliant adulthood. However, if we fail to provide a rite of passage—including preparation, event, and celebration—that recasts the kids' lives as they break free from their mothers' and fathers' direct influence, they end up drifting, drifting . . . possibly even stuck in outer space (or in their childhood bedrooms).

The good news is that we can learn to help our kids take advantage of the slingshot effect. This allows them to stop depending on their parents for their choices, decisions, and needs. In fact, this essential experience frees them by helping them change their focus and gain the momentum they need to reach responsible, capable adulthood. We can picture it, using the illustration on the following page.

The horizontal arrow in diagram 8 represents a rite of passage event that moves kids from childhood to adulthood. First, on the top (childhood) side of the diagram, you equip your children. As you teach and train them (rite of passage preparation), they acquire more and more of the skills they need for self-reliant living and take on more and more adult responsibilities. This training helps them accelerate toward the rite of passage event—the line on the diagram—which effectively slingshots them into life as emerging adults, the lower portion of the diagram. A public acknowledgement of what has occurred through rite of passage preparation and event is the rite of passage celebration, a formal recognition by family and friends that the children have crossed the line into adulthood.

RITE OF PASSAGE PARENTING

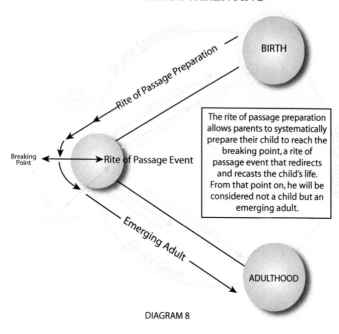

DIAGRAM 8

> ⟿ **EMERGING ADULTS:** Young people who have experienced a rite of passage and gradually assume full adult responsibilities and adult consequences.
>
> ⟿ **RITE OF PASSAGE PARENTS:** Parents who lead their child toward capable, responsible, self-reliant adulthood by providing ways to bring closure to childhood and experience a rite of passage.

At this point, emerging adults don't run back to the bedroom or seek out their hovering helicopter parents. Rite of passage preparation has equipped them well, and they accelerate toward their ultimate destination of adulthood by accepting adult responsibilities and facing adult consequences *on their own*. They respond as capable, responsible emerging adults.

Like all of us, they still make mistakes, and they are still learning, but they do not return to their childhood. Like Jesus in Jerusalem, they know they have crossed the line into adulthood by experiencing a meaningful rite of passage event.

⤳

THE PRINCIPLE OF EXPECTATION STATES THAT THE THOUGHTS AND IDEAS PLANTED IN AN INDIVIDUAL'S MIND HELP GUIDE HIS FUTURE DEVELOPMENT.

Parents, I hear you: "I don't live in Jerusalem—and I'm certainly not raising Jesus." How do we give our McDonald's Kids a rite of passage? How do we recast their lives toward responsible adulthood? I'll spend the rest of this book equipping you to fix it by becoming Rite of Passage Parents. Let's begin with the basics.

THE PRINCIPLE OF EXPECTATION

The *Principle of Expectation* states that the thoughts and ideas planted in an individual's mind help guide his future development. If you want to become a Rite of Passage Parent, you have to cast positive expectations into your kids' lives so you can call forth a rite of passage later. From the time your children are born (or as soon as you understand these truths), you need to talk to them, casting into their lives the goal of capable, responsible, self-reliant adulthood.

You do this by assuring them that there will come a day when they will grow up. In fact, they have already grown much less dependent upon you than they were at birth. Right now, you explain, you provide for many of their basic needs. You buy their food and clothes. You provide the car they ride in and the place where they live. Someday, they will buy the things they need . . . all by themselves. They will now learn to drive and maintain their own cars, and they'll have their own homes. As responsible adults, they'll take care of all these areas and more—completely on their own. You want to help prepare them to make wise decisions in the future by gradually building their skills, abilities, and responsibilities today.

By having these conversations with your children—and you should have them again and again as they grow—you are preparing them for the day when you recast their lives toward responsible adulthood. If you like, you can even use the example of the lunar slingshot to tell them about the way they'll accelerate by acquiring skills and responsibilities, reach a breaking point, change direction, and then slingshot away from their childhood dependency and on into adult responsibilities and adult consequences. You can affirm your child's desire to grow up by beginning, as soon as you can, this rite of passage preparation.

THE RITE OF PASSAGE EVENT

In the United States, one of the reasons we have trouble casting a positive expectation and calling forth responsible adulthood from our kids is because we have never identified an event that will help them say, "Look at me. I'm doing adult things; therefore, I'm an adult." Like Johnny with his basket of adult activities, young people are searching for this event to mark their transition to mature adulthood.

What, specifically, is a rite of passage event? The event itself will vary from family to family, and from child to child. Parents can best determine an activity that will call forth adulthood for a particular child, moving him or her away from comfort zones and into adult responsibilities. In order to serve as a genuine rite of passage event, its scope should extend well beyond that of a required class project or church- or school-mandated service project. Examples include:

- Organizing and supervising a project at a homeless shelter
- Setting up and administering a tutoring program for an elementary school
- Planning and carrying out an activity to raise money for a cause

RITE OF PASSAGE PARENTING

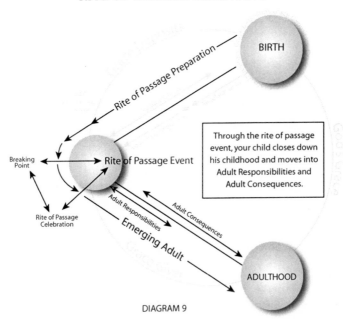

BIRTH

Rite of Passage Preparation

Breaking Point

Rite of Passage Event

Rite of Passage Celebration

Adult Responsibilities

Adult Consequences

Emerging Adult

Through the rite of passage event, your child closes down his childhood and moves into Adult Responsibilities and Adult Consequences.

ADULTHOOD

DIAGRAM 9

In each case, the child should handle all the details of the event, going beyond mere participation (childlike behavior) to initiation, organization, and execution (adult responsibility).

I believe that the ultimate rite of passage event is one in which the student crosses cultural boundaries to take on adult responsibilities and adult consequences. In the Christian world, I would suggest a cross-cultural mission trip, particularly one that has been purposefully designed to build adult skills into participants' lives.

In order to experience a genuine rite of passage event, kids must leave the parental realm of control. From this point forward, we reset our kids' mental clock so that they no longer perceive themselves as children but as emerging adults. Their parents must also think differently, using positive expectations to call forth adult responsibilities.

RITE OF PASSAGE CELEBRATION

After the rite of passage event calls forth your child's adulthood, a rite of passage celebration displays its evidence for your child, your family, and everyone else who witnesses this memorable time. Rite of passage parents will cast the expectation far ahead of time for this milestone, which tells the world that the emerging adult has accomplished specific steps.

The rite of passage celebration should take place when your child is thirteen to fifteen years old. Those who participate in it will see clearly that this child has earned the right to move into adulthood—to become more dependent on God and self than parents. Rite of Passage Parents enable their kids to reach this point through rite of passage preparation. Section Two of this book discusses the specifics of giving your kids incremental tasks that will propel this process.

Many parents mark their children's growth on a door, wall, or special chart. They enjoy periodically checking these marks and measuring the children against them. In the same way, rite of passage parents will know whether their kids are ready for their rite of passage event and celebration by measuring them against certain marks of responsibility. These marks, as explained here, show that kids have what it takes to act like adults.

FILLING LITTLE JOHNNY'S BASKET: FIVE MARKS

Do you remember Little Johnny, running around collecting adult activities to put into his basket? The book of 1 Timothy contains a verse that gives us a great definition of the other side of the rite of passage event and shows how people know that Little Johnny is really an adult: "Do not let anyone treat you as if you are unimportant because you are young. Instead, be an example to the believers with your words, your actions, your love, your faith, and your pure life" (1 Tim. 4:12 NCV). That verse sets forth five key marks that help us prepare a child for a rite of passage.

At just ten years of age, Jesus would have had to memorize the first five books of the Bible in their entirety. That was his *beth zaphar*, one of the marks of maturity that Jewish culture imposed upon its members at that time. Similarly, we need to place marks into our children's lives that help them move toward a rite of passage event and celebration. These steps are an important part of rite of passage preparation. They help us prepare kids' hearts and lives for the journey toward capable, responsible, self-reliant adulthood.

MARK #1: WORDS

When our children are tiny, they speak as we expect little children to speak. We wait eagerly for that first "Da-da" or "Ma-ma," applauding it when it comes. But as our children grow and mature, we need to encourage them to move toward adult speech.

As we've discussed, our culture has shifted dramatically;

in the process, our children have experienced losses. Kids today are more comfortable getting *online* than staying *in line*. Today's high school and college students are the first generation that grew up seeing pictures of missing children on milk cartons, the first told never to talk to strangers, the first that spent more hours inside in front of a computer than outside playing with siblings. In fact, our increasing technological abilities have eroded our kids' speaking skills.

I can often gauge the level of a student's maturity simply by the way he communicates. At twelve years of age, Jesus sat in the temple and dialogued with the "lawyers of lawyers." He knew how to ask the right questions, gather information, process what he heard, and interact intelligently with the other adults who surrounded him.

The adolescent language known as *teenspeak* is another false rite of passage for today's generation. Students talk and text-message in an ever-changing code that baffles adults. Using words that adults don't understand gives them a sense of control. Subgroups of teens even change the meaning of the code words, creating an inner circle and alienating other teenagers.

Neither John-Boy nor Jesus needed teenspeak to empower him. Each had experienced a rite of passage and had taken on adult responsibilities. Each was able to communicate with other adults as an adult. I know you're an adult when you put away childish things, including your speech (see 1 Corinthians 13:11).

> ◆ Teenspeak: Coded language used by the teenage subgroup as a means of empowerment.

Mark #2: Actions

This area of rite of passage preparation covers behavior. In the second chapter of Luke, Jesus submitted himself to his authorities in the temple, acting as an adult. McDonald's Kids don't behave like this, and as a result, many businesses don't want youth groups coming anywhere near! In fact, hotel employees often call church groups "teenagers from hell" because they run up and down the hallways, slamming doors and screaming. Restaurants hate it when these same groups visit on Wednesday nights or Sunday afternoons, because the kids never seem to display adult conduct there, either. Can you imagine Grandpa running around the dining area, yelling at the top of his lungs, or Grandma using her straw to blow spit wads at her best friend?

Of course not! These tricks are for kids.

I know you're an adult when you begin to conduct yourself in an acceptable, appropriate manner.

Mark #3: Love

The kind of love that demonstrates readiness for adulthood is selfless, not a childish love that only considers "me" and "mine." Grown-up love puts other people's needs first. Young people today want their families to scrimp and save so they can have an iPod or join their friends on the senior-high ski trip. These McDonald's Kids expect their parents to make sacrifices on their behalf—but they rarely intend to surrender their own wants in order to help someone else.

My son Jeremiah demonstrated an adult love when his grandmother became ill with cancer. As a junior and new transfer student at Hannibal-LaGrange College, he took on the adult responsibility of caring for his grandmother for the final nine months before she went to heaven.

During this time, Jeremiah lived in Grandma's home, took care of her house and yard, drove her to doctor's appointments, and met many of her other needs. He even bought her a little bell to ring whenever she needed his help, and spent much of his time outside class making sure she was comfortable.

By doing these things, Jeremiah demonstrated an adult love. Adult love understands that sometimes the needs of others outweigh our own. Adult love also understands that the needs of the many sometimes outweigh the needs of the one—even if it means waiting awhile before you get that cell phone or MP3 player.

I know you're ready for a rite of passage event
when you make decisions ensuring that others' needs are
met before your own.

Mark #4: Faithfulness

Many people believe that this area of maturity refers to faith or religion. Instead, it comes from a word that means faithfulness (or fidelity). Faithfulness means that if I give you a job, I can count on you to complete it. You are a trustworthy person. If you give me your word, I know you will do as you said you would. However, faithfulness is not something our McDonald's Kids seem to value.

Once upon a time, the older demons gave the younger demons an assignment: find something to make the youth minister go crazy—something to make his job a living example of their evil domain. They gathered for a brainstorming session.

One of the demons said, "How about an all-night lock-in?"

The rest chimed in, "No, we tried that. The youth pastor got wise to it."

Another demon said, "How about a bake sale?"

They all chimed in again, "Been there, done that, got the brownies."

Then the youngest demon spoke up. "How about a car wash?"

They all said, "That is *so* last summer!"

Their young friend responded, "I know, but this time, we'll make sure the kids don't show up for it!"

So the innocent youth pastor worked hard and put together a car wash to raise money for homeless people. He had thirty kids signed up to help. Bright and early Saturday morning, our brave young minister was ready. He rose at daybreak, left his family sleeping, and stood in the church parking lot at 7:00 a.m. with buckets, hoses, sponges, and soap—but no students.

Finally, at 7:30, he decided to call one of the leadership team members to find out where he was. "You were supposed to be here," the youth pastor said. "You made a commitment!"

The student responded, somewhat sleepily, "Oh, I had something else—our soccer team practices on Saturday morning, too. I knew I couldn't do both, so I chose soccer."

The demons chuckled. They had been successful in getting the students to make *many* commitments for the same Saturday morning, knowing that no one would choose the car wash. They rubbed their hands together in glee. Not only had they ruined the car wash, but they had also been successful in changing the meaning of the word *commitment*.

This generation gathers multiple commitments and then decides which, if any, to honor. Because of this tendency, I now use the word *surrender* rather than *commitment*. I ask students if they will *surrender* to a particular task or ministry. Today's young people allow *commitments* to change, but *surrender* . . . they seem to understand that.

I know you're an adult
when you can be trusted to surrender to a task or ministry.

MARK #5: PURE LIFE

The final way young people show they are ready for a rite of passage event is through their pure lives. Instead of encouraging students to master their hormones, the Enemy tries to make hormones the master of their lives. You see it everywhere: the world constantly makes excuses for the increasingly immoral behavior of young people.

Pure lives are essential because we don't want the messenger to get in the way of the message. For example, if someone tries to tell how wonderful God is but has an impure lifestyle, the message disappears. We need to encourage our kids to discipline all five areas of their lives so that the message shines through them each day.

I know you're an adult when you demonstrate moral purity,
and the message shines through your life.

WHAT ARE THE ODDS?

Jesus was the Master of many things, but one of them was the principle of positive expectations. Early on in his ministry, he told his disciples many things that were not *yet* true about them but *would be* true one day.

As I grew up, this principle of positive expectations weighed heavily upon me, because the expectations others projected onto me were anything but positive. A sign in front of my school reads Slow. Children. I always thought it referred to me! I had a speech impediment, and I stayed on the *slow row* in the classroom. Because I perceived myself as slow, I acted that way. Getting good grades was always a problem for me, and from my earliest days, nearly everyone I knew gave me the impression that I would never accomplish very much.

One day, God brought along someone who constantly put positive expectations into my life. This person was a Sunday school teacher named Clyde Lionberger. He was my teacher during those critical junior high years.

Every time I was around Clyde, he told me that one day I was going to do something great. Clyde even told me that someday I was going to be a preacher! No one else was telling me those things; in fact, most of them were busy doing just the opposite.

To me, Clyde was like Jesus: he believed in me when there was nothing much to see. Incredibly, he saw something of worth in little Walker Moore and used his positive words to call it forth. Because of his influence, I came to believe that I was a person of worth and value.

As Rite of Passage Parents, we need to exercise caution about what we put into the minds of our children. After all, we are the guardians of these minds, and we need to protect our kids' thoughts from any dangerous input: our own speech, the words of other people, or the barrage of media that blasts through their world every day. The Enemy wants them to think that they're losers who will never make it. We give our kids the expectation of failure when we say things like, "You never do anything right!" or "Can't you ever think for yourself?" People live up to our expectations—positive or negative —nearly every time.

Jesus wisely and carefully planted ideas in his followers' minds that would one day bear wholesome fruit. When his disciples looked like nothing but a bunch of bumbling idiots, he cast into them the positive expectation that they would do greater things than he had: "Most assuredly, I say to you, he who believes in me, the works that I do he will do also; and greater works than these he will do, because I go to my Father" (John 14:12 NKJV).

The people who knew these men must have laughed. "He's

walked on water; he's healed people; he's multiplied a tiny bit of food to feed thousands of people. How are *they* going to do more than *he* did?"

These bumbling idiots were the same ones that God used to develop the early church and began the movement that later "turned the world upside down" (Acts 17:6 NKJV) by taking the gospel to the nations. What are the odds that a group of "losers" would accomplish such great things? Probably the same odds that someone who had such great difficulty reading and speaking as a boy would one day travel the world, speak to thousands of people each year, and write books about parenting. When Jesus enters the picture, the odds don't matter. They're always 100 percent.

From Boy to Man

As we prepare our kids for a rite of passage, parents have a responsibility to cast positive expectations into their kids' lives. They should know that we expect them to live and act as emerging adults. "Ha! Not *my* teenagers," you may be tempted to say.

You know, you're exactly right. Most kids today haven't had the opportunity to experience a rite of passage. Our culture has deprived almost all of them of this essential step. But what do you think could happen if one of today's McDonald's Kids went through a genuine rite of passage?

I know the answer to that question, because I see it happen all the time. Let me tell you of the impact that a rite of passage event had on just one young man who served with Awe Star Ministries during two consecutive summers.

During training, I always tell our students that I can't take teenagers overseas—and I can't. Can you imagine having to deal with McDonald's Kids in a McDavid's culture? The dangers of this situation have led me to cast the vision for adulthood into each student's life before we ever put him on a plane or take her across a border.

I teach students that, before they leave training, they need to lay down their childhood and willingly take on adult responsibilities. In fact, laying down their adolescence is a critical part of the students' overall experience. The point when they step away from childhood serves as (you guessed it) a rite of passage event.

Over the years, we have seen God do some amazing things as students work through their rites of passage. One of these students was a young man named Brent Higgins Jr., known as "BJ." In June 2004, BJ arrived at our training camp, Awe Star University, for the first time. At fourteen, he was the youngest and, at five feet two inches tall and just over one hundred pounds, the smallest student who served with us that summer.

BJ was set to travel to Peru as part of a drama team, and he joined us for a time of training for this cross-cultural work. When I asked the students, as I do before every trip, which of them would be willing to put aside childish attitudes and actions in order to embrace adulthood, BJ was the first to accept the challenge. This decision changed his life forever. The following e-mail, which he sent from Peru, shows the significance of this experience:

Sent: Wednesday, June 30, 2004, 10:05 a.m.
Subject: To my family

Hey guys! I'm in Piura right now; we arrived last night. I'm having an awesome time here. I love all my team members and everyone else that was at training—there are so many awesome people. I can't wait to tell you about them all!

When I come back, I will not be the little boy that you dropped off all by himself at the airport. Two nights before we left for Peru there was a sermon entitled "Missions: Danger, For Adults Only." It was explained that this new Western culture of how we're children, then adolescents from nine through twenty-six, then adults is completely wrong. . . . Walker used several Scriptures to explain that biblically, and in God's will, you go from child to adult through one thing. One rite of passage [event]. . . . Then he went on to explain that we couldn't afford adolescents on the mission field. We needed to step up and . . . become adults.

At the end of the sermon he said, "Those of you who feel it's time . . . [to] start to live, lead, serve, and act like adults, stand up so that I can pray with you." Having just earlier that evening, before the sermon, prayed that God would change me from boy to man, because I knew I could not lead in my team or minister in Peru as this boy that I had always only been, I was the first to stand up, then several around me stood as well. . . . So, long story short, when I come back, you will not find the boy you knew, but a man in his place.[2]

At fourteen years of age, BJ embraced his manhood. Throughout his time in Peru, he showed that he knew how to handle the adult responsibilities and adult consequences he faced each day. Even though every one of his teammates was older than he was, they all recognized him as their leader.

When BJ returned home, his family, although skeptical at first, gradually came to realize that what he had written earlier was true: BJ had given up his childhood through this rite of passage event and become a man. They honored him with a rite of passage celebration on his fifteenth birthday just a few months later, pronouncing his manhood and presenting him with the symbolic gift of a sword. BJ wrote about this meaningful experience in his online journal:

> Now, for the bigger, more serious side of the gift—as he gave it to me, my dad said, "This sword is symbolizing your coming into adulthood." It is this profound statement from my father that makes the sword, though small in size, bigger in value than even my wicked awesome stereo. It is not just that I really, really wanted a sword 'cause they're cool, but that my dad presented it to me, announcing his blessing on my coming into manhood. With the exception of the gifts that God himself directly gives, one could not ask for a greater gift.[3]

BJ and his family understood: one of the greatest needs in a child's life is parents who provide closure to childhood through a rite of passage. The combination of rite of passage preparation, a rite of passage event, and a rite of passage celebration give them peace and contentment in their identity.

If you don't get a grip on Rite of Passage Parenting, your children will struggle with deep questions ("When do I grow up? Who am I going to be?") for the rest of their lives. This essential experience answers these questions. Rites of passage are integral to their purpose, their identity, their reason for being on this earth. If you don't give them the key, they will not be able to unlock the door to capable, responsible, self-reliant adulthood and step into fulfilling, meaningful lives.

⊰ RITE OF PASSAGE PARENTING SUMMARY ⊱

God has placed within each of our children the deep-seated desire to grow up. Rite of Passage Parenting uses a rite of passage to move children into adulthood. The process is comparable to the lunar slingshot that rocket scientists use to increase the acceleration and recast the course of a spacecraft.

As children move through the rite of passage preparation, they gradually take on more adult responsibilities. Eventually, they reach the breaking point where they are ready for a rite of passage event that recasts their lives. Afterward, a rite of passage celebration acknowledges their emerging adulthoods. Five marks of maturity (see 1 Timothy 4:12) prepare a child for a rite of passage and indicate his or her readiness for adulthood: words, actions, love, faithfulness, and purity.

SIGNIFICANT
TASKS

〜

CHAPTER FOUR

WHAT'S MISSING:
KIDS NEED SIGNIFICANT TASKS

Unlike past generations, where kids performed real work that mattered, today's kids have no true significant tasks—special assignments that demonstrate their worth to the people who are important to them.

When I was a youth minister, I learned one important fact very quickly. In church work, youth pastors rank at the bottom of the pay scale. First comes the pastor, then the minister of music, then the minister of education, then the janitor, and then . . . the youth pastor.

Because of this well-known truth, church members occasionally took pity on me. In one church, a deacon even gave me a car. Of course, this was after he figured out that no dealer would take it for a trade-in. In a move calculated for maximum spiritual impact, he blessed our family with his extra vehicle.

Like many of the offerings given to the church or its staff, this one needed more than a little help. It was always breaking down, and I always needed to work on it. One day I was underneath the car, tinkering away in an effort to fix something else that had gone awry. I heard a little voice tentatively calling out, "Dad."

I looked up and saw Caleb's scrawny four-year-old legs squatting down beside me. His head was turned sideways as he peered into the darkness, trying to figure out what his dad was doing under the car. His blue eyes gazed trustingly into mine. "Dad, can I help?"

At least he wasn't offering to sell me a free apartment guide. At first I was tempted to tell him, "No. There's nothing you can really do. Just let me get to work, son—that's about all the help you can give me until you get a whole lot bigger."

This wasn't what I said, however. There are at least a few times when I get it right. "Caleb!" I said as in amazement. "I am *so glad* you came along just now. You see, my tools keep rolling away from me every time I set them down. Do you think you could hold this screwdriver so I don't lose it, son?"

"Oh *yes*, Dad. I can do that!"

Caleb clasped the tool close to his chest, holding on to it tightly in his eagerness to assist me. Every few minutes, I would take the screwdriver from his sweaty hands, reach up underneath the car, and make a bunch of important-sounding noises.

About this time, Cathy came walking by. Caleb could hardly wait to share his important news. "Look, Mom! *I'm helping Dad!*"

Later, when I thought I had banged around sufficiently and maybe even solved whatever problem the car had that time, Caleb and I went inside. The first thing he did was climb up on a chair beside his mother and puff out his little chest, announcing, "Mom, I helped Dad fix the car!"

We may smile, but we also understand: those few minutes in the garage meant a lot to Caleb. Even at a young age, he wanted to have a vital, important part in his family. He wanted what I call a *significant task*.

WHERE'S THE TASK?

Parents, let me ask you a question: What does your child do that demonstrates her worth and adds value to your family? If she were away today and unable to perform this assignment, how much would your family suffer? If you struggle to come up with an answer, your child is probably missing significant tasks.

Caleb was not alone in his desire for a significant task. Just as we have a need deep within us to experience a rite of passage, we also have a need to feel important, to have an assignment that shows our value to the group in which we live. In fact, if we don't complete this significant task, others will suffer.

> ❖ SIGNIFICANT TASK: A special assignment that demonstrates an individual's worth to the people he considers important.

By its nature, an agricultural society gives every child significant tasks that make him or her feel important and valued. In fact, the children in agricultural societies typically earn money for the family through their contribution to the collective work. Today, we often see statistics about the overwhelming costs of raising just one child. Parents of more than two or three recognize the rolled eyes and the superior tone: "You have *how many* kids?"

Prior to the agricultural-industrial cultural shift, however, the average child brought his family the equivalent of five thousand dollars in annual income. Back then, children were a necessity, not a luxury, because they quickly learned practical skills and took on important responsibilities. In an agricultural society, children are economic assets, and the man who has many is rich.

Let's return to our good friend John-Boy. Today, he is back in his right mind, no longer using teenspeak or wearing bling-bling and low-riding jeans. As we mentioned, John and Olivia Walton had some unusual ideas about what kids ought to do with their time. John-Boy and each of his brothers and sisters were given chores, or significant tasks. One of John-Boy's jobs was chopping wood. What would have happened if John-Boy hadn't chopped the wood?

If John-Boy hadn't chopped the wood, the fire would have gone out. Grandma and Olivia wouldn't have been able to cook the family meals on the big, old-fashioned woodstove, and the Waltons would have had no fuel to heat their home.

Of course, John-Boy wasn't the only one who had important jobs. One of Mary Ellen's significant tasks was milking the family cow. What would have happened if Mary Ellen had chosen not to complete this significant task?

At one conference, when I posed this question to a group of parents, one man excitedly raised his hand, ready with an answer. I figured he had come from a rural background and was going to fill us in about all the dangers that go along with unmilked cows. He could hardly wait for me to call on him as he blurted out, "The cow would explode?"

After we all stopped laughing, I told him the truth. No, the cow wouldn't have exploded, but she would have been very uncomfortable, and eventually she would have stopped giving milk. The Waltons' milk supply would literally have dried up until the cow delivered another calf and her body made more milk to meet the needs of her baby (as well as the Walton family).

When our society made the relatively quick switch from agricultural to industrial, we not only stopped giving each of our kids a rite of passage, we also stopped giving them significant tasks. Families with five or six kids moved into suburbia and realized that their children no longer had important roles to perform.

In the 1950s, parents welcomed the idea that their kids had easier lives than they did as children. And for the first time, a generation grew up whining about boredom: "There's nothing to do around here." These kids had lost their purpose. They had lost their function within the family. They had lost their significant tasks.

Work It Out

When I was growing up, a friend from the city came out to visit us overnight on our farm in Missouri. We got up early, as all farmers do, and went out to take care of the livestock. Our friend went with us. We checked the pigs, replenished the feeding troughs, undid bales of hay for the cattle, and filled empty water tanks, arriving back at the house just in time for breakfast.

I HAVE LEARNED THROUGH THE YEARS THAT WHEN I ASK SOMEONE, "WHAT DO YOU DO?" THE ANSWER IS HIS OR HER SIGNIFICANT TASK: "I'M A MOTHER." "I'M AN ATTORNEY." "I'M A FIREFIGHTER." "I'M A TEACHER." IN THIS WAY, WHAT YOU *DO* DEFINES WHO YOU ARE.

At the table, our city friend announced to my dad, "That sure was hard work." My dad looked at him in amazement. Bluntly, he told him, "No, son. We've done our *chores*. After breakfast . . . we go to *work*."

Chores were significant tasks. Although my brothers and I

didn't always appreciate them at the time, these significant tasks showed us that we were important, taught us practical skills for living, and built in us a lasting work ethic.

I have learned through the years that when I ask someone, "What do you do?" the answer is his or her significant task: "I'm a mother." "I'm an attorney." "I'm a firefighter." "I'm a teacher." In this way, what you *do* defines who you are.

I often try talking to students about their significant tasks. When I ask them what they do that makes them valuable to their families, they seem puzzled. Eventually, I almost always get the same two responses: "I make my bed." "I take out the trash."

The Baby Boomers—the first generation to grow up without significant tasks—have now produced a second generation lacking this essential element. We somehow lost the idea that kids can perform valuable functions that add value both to family life and to their own lives. Sure, mom and dad may become impatient if Little Johnny doesn't make his bed or take out the trash, but no one will suffer anything more than temporary inconvenience.

> For most of our history, the labor of young people in their teens was too important to be sacrificed. Europeans observed that Americans grew quickly in every way, taking on responsibilities and vices much sooner than their European counterparts . . . While having a teenager in the household once gave parents useful labor and even a positive cash flow, contemporary teens are far more often a financial drain.[1]

Countless movies and television shows feature rites of passage. However, significant tasks have also earned media attention. In *The Lord of the Rings: The Fellowship of the Ring*, the hero, Frodo Baggins (Elijah Wood), has a decision to make regarding his significant task. He has been entrusted with an ancient ring, and the fate of the entire world depends on his journey across Middle-earth to destroy it. He chooses to accept his assignment, beginning a quest to cast the magical ring of power into the dark fires of Mount Doom. The movie tells the story of Frodo and his brave band (the Fellowship of the Ring) as he works to carry out his significant task. Destroying the ring showed Frodo's value—to the others in The Fellowship, and to his entire world.

What draws so many people to movies like this? Why do they have such amazing appeal? They attract us because we can live vicariously through the characters and identify with the challenges they face. We all need rites of passage and significant tasks. Movies such as *Star Wars* and *The Lord of the Rings* address these God-given needs and encourage us to fulfill them in our own lives. We enjoy watching others navigate the essential experiences that, deep down, we all crave.

When television first became popular back in the 1950s, most of the programs featured young people who were seeking their significant tasks. If Theodore "Beaver" Cleaver of *Leave it to Beaver* had been born during the Waltons' era, for example, he would not have been running around the neighborhood . . . and he certainly would have been too busy to get into trouble with his sneaky friend, Eddie Haskell.

In the same way, almost all of Lucy's frequent—and funny— antics in *I Love Lucy* featured her search for a significant task. Desi was the bandleader at the Tropicana; Desi received frequent invitations to travel and perform—but where was Lucy? Out stomping grapes, or trying to sell "Vitameatavegamin," or somehow finding new ways to convince Ricky to let her appear on stage with him just *once*.

What really makes us laugh about *I Love Lucy*? Her hilarious attempts to fulfill her longing for significant tasks. Every day, people do ludicrous things to let the world know they have something unique to offer. They want to show that they have significant tasks.

Pseudo-Significant Tasks

Since God has placed within us the desire for significant tasks, what happens if we don't have any? We create what *Rite of Passage Parenting* calls *pseudo-significant tasks*, activities that outwardly appear to be meaningful but have no intrinsic value.

Again, our friend Little Johnny makes a good example. Little Johnny and his friends grew up in suburban America in the 1950s. Unlike his dad, who spent his childhood days on a farm, Little Johnny had no corn to plant, cows to milk, or wood to chop. Since Little Johnny and his friends were part of the first generation raised without significant tasks, they had to invent ways of feeling important. In response to this need in their lives, Little Johnny and his friends created the '60s.

> ◆ Pseudo-Significant Tasks: Activities that outwardly appear to be meaningful but have no intrinsic value.

Little Johnny's generation found its sense of worth by standing on the side of the road holding signs that screamed, "Make Love, Not War." They wore peace signs around their necks, plastered them on the bumpers of their cars, and flashed them with two fingers to anyone who even looked as though he might be paying attention. They held sit-ins and lock-ins and all sorts of other -*ins* as they tried to make themselves heard in their families and in society.

Did you know that the Coca-Cola Company wrote a song for Little Johnny? They called it, "I'd Like to Teach the World to Sing." This song about spreading peace and harmony described the things Little Johnny and his friends identified as their significant tasks. They held hands across the fields and sang the song as their own special anthem. This generation listened to its own music, made up its own rules, and marched to a different drummer . . . I think his name was Ringo Starr.

Little Johnny and his friends of the '60s era were doing exactly what kids do today because their society and their families fail to provide them with significant tasks. In order to keep their sanity, they took on pseudo-significant tasks that have no real value.

Unfortunately, many people have resigned themselves to pseudo-significant tasks. Like the movie sets on the back lots of Hollywood, these false tasks present a solid outward appearance. However, when you look behind them, you see there is no real mansion, no real store, and no real significant task.

We all present a false front from time to time. We may continue telling ourselves that our pseudo-significant tasks are real and important—but like the false fronts, they will eventually fall. God has built the desire for meaning into our lives, and we cannot live with the knowledge that the things we do lack value and purpose.

Do you know what stopped the '60s? The '70s! Little Johnny got married. What's marriage? A significant task. No longer could Little Johnny run up and down the highways carrying signs that said, "Stop the War." After all, his wife expected him to come home for dinner. Little Johnny got a job—a significant task. Next, he and his wife began to have children—you guessed it, a *very* significant task.

Suddenly, Little Johnny didn't have time to sing about peace and harmony. Instead, he had to go to work to make money to buy that pink fluid that sat in his refrigerator day in and day out to fight sore throats and throbbing ears. He had to buy clothes and diapers. He had to pay the electric bill and put gas in the car. Little Johnny no longer needed those pseudo-significant tasks because his tasks were so . . . significant.

Bus-ted

As late as the 1950s, society still provided young people with some significant tasks. In South Carolina and several other states, you could get a driver's license as young as age fourteen. One man tells about being responsible for an entire school bus route . . . at only sixteen years old. He would park the bus in front of his house each night, leaving for school very early in the morning so he could pick up a group of elementary school children and deliver them to a school across town.

In order to qualify for this significant task, this man and his fellow student bus drivers took a special summer class sponsored by the South Carolina State Highway Patrol. After they had completed the textbook portion of the course, a patrolman rode alongside them in the bus, watching their driving and correcting their mistakes as they took turns at the wheel.

Would we entrust any of our McDonald's Kids with the responsibility of a bus route? I doubt it. However, in the mid-1950s, this same group of students had the distinction of earning a higher safety rating than any team of school bus drivers in the state.[2] These young people had wholeheartedly embraced their significant task.

History Lessons

We no longer consider teenagers, or even young adults, a responsible part of society. What happened? Yes, you guessed it—our culture shifted.

> In the 1930s, most children were enthusiastic about finding ways to improve their lot in life. Because life was hard, they grew up fast and had to become self-reliant. Because they were needed and considered important assets, they usually made significant contributions to their family's well-being. . . . After World War II, life changed drastically. America's growing affluence began to encourage self-indulgence. By the 1960s, a growing number of children, who no longer felt needed as contributors and had little encouragement to be self-reliant, began to lose direction in their preparation for life. (They had not had to put forth much effort to contribute and cooperate in the family. Why start now?)[3]

Our culture changed, and with it, so did our perceptions about what young people could and should accomplish. Certainly, we're not the first parents to struggle with the idea of allowing our kids to assume adult responsibilities. After all, we're raising them, and we know (or think we know) what they can and can't do.

Remember Jesus in Jerusalem, staying behind to dialogue with the teachers in the temple? At first, his parents didn't understand his actions either. Somehow, they may not have realized exactly how important his significant task really was.

CALEB AND THE GRAPE KOOL-AID

This same thing happened at our house more than once. On one occasion, just days after we had installed new beige Berber carpeting in our dining room, six-year-old Caleb saw that the pitcher of Mom's famous Kool-Aid needed to reach the dinner table. The flavor of the day was grape.

"Can I help?" he asked his mother.

Like any good mother, Cathy thought immediately of the new beige carpet and the fact that she had filled the pitcher nearly to the brim. Right there in the kitchen, she had one of those déjà vu moments every parent dreads. Her mind instantly pictured the deep purple liquid arcing through the air, splattering our son, the table, and . . . the brand-new carpet.

"No thanks, honey, I'll take care of it," she responded, hurrying to take the pitcher. "Just go sit down and watch television until dinner is ready."

As I watched the scene, I couldn't understand why our youngest son suddenly seemed so upset. Hadn't Cathy just helped him by carrying the too-full pitcher of Kool-Aid? Wasn't he now parked in front of his favorite cartoon?

A rare flash of insight helped me see what had really occurred. When Caleb asked, "Can I help?" he was looking for a significant task—exactly what any other child who asks this question is seeking. You see, Caleb knew that carrying the Kool-Aid—as dangerous as it might be to beige carpet— was a task more significant than watching cartoons.

What happened in our home that evening reflects what we, as parents, have inadvertently done with this generation. We have told our kids to "go sit down and watch television" while we carry out the important work of family life. Later, when they're older and, we believe, more capable, we suddenly ask them to take on things we consider *real* significant tasks. No wonder they roll their eyes and effectively tell us, "No way." For years, we've been training them to think that they can't do anything truly significant.

SIGNIFICANT FUN

I think I know how Caleb felt. As I mentioned, I grew up living in the country, and then moved to the inner city. Later, Mom and Dad moved us back out to the country. That last move may have had something to do with those forty slashed tires . . . they never really said.

During our years in the city, I especially loved going to visit my grandparents' farm. Why? They let me have significant tasks! At Grandma and Grandpa's, I helped drive the tractor, "buck" bales (a special way of flipping bales of hay from the field to a wagon or barn), plant corn, and herd the cattle to take them to auction. Grandpa even let me bid for him at the auctions by holding up his special "auction cane" when he gave the signal. After he died, I received this cane. Today, it is propped beside my front door.

I didn't know that my grandparents were helping me find a place of worth and value in my family by letting me perform significant tasks. I just thought I was having fun!

Today, parents seem to think our primary responsibility is to entertain our kids. Instead of providing them with meaningful work, we try to make them happy by buying them the newest Nintendo systems, CDs, DVDs, MP3s, and TVs for their bedrooms—then wonder why they never want to leave. Jane Adams, social psychologist and author of *When Our Grown Kids Disappoint Us*, notes the following:

It must have been easier for our own parents, who didn't worry the way we do about making their kids happy . . . What distinguishes baby-boom parents from those of earlier generations is how much importance we place on our kids' inner psychological qualities as well as their educational and occupational success, moral and ethical values, and satisfaction in their relationships.[4]

Living Beyond Ourselves

When I had my ten-year anniversary as a youth minister, my students held a reunion for all the kids who had grown up under my care. I like to think I'm a pretty decent communicator, so while I had all these students together, I asked them which Bible study I had taught had changed their lives the most.

"Was it the one about Jesus + Nothing = Everything? Was it the one about living the lifestyle of a missionary? Was it . . . ?" I pressed them, trying to find answers that would help me learn more about the impact of my work and what I might need to change.

The room grew deathly quiet. The young people looked, as we said when I was growing up on the farm, "like a cow at a new gate." Finally, one brave young man spoke up, "I can't say I remember much about the Bible studies, Walker. What meant the most to me was when you took us over the border. Remember that time we went to Mexico and slept on dirt floors?"

Others began chiming in. "Yeah. Remember when we worked with the people who lived on the garbage dump?"

"Remember when we learned that drama and shared it at the Plaza in Nuevo Laredo? So many people came to know the Lord!"

I realized that it wasn't my brilliant teaching, after all, that had touched and changed their lives. Instead, it was (you guessed it) the way the Lord had led me to provide them with opportunities for significant tasks.

These students had come a long way from the selfish attitudes and actions of McDonald's Kids. Through their cross-cultural service, they had accomplished significant tasks that had taught them to think beyond their own needs, adding meaning and purpose to their lives.

Years ago, before the agricultural-industrial cultural shift, this attitude was much more common. Kids from previous generations did not typically have their own bedrooms—certainly not the kind that come equipped with a personal television, computer, and CD player. They did not have wardrobes that required revamping every season to match the latest styles.

Our old friends the Waltons lived this way as well. Their everyday family life made it natural for John-Boy to grow up thinking about "we" rather than "me." He was able to sacrifice his own time and desires when necessary because he knew his family needed him. In turn, they willingly extended the same loving concern to him. If you grow up believing you're the center of the universe, you never look beyond yourself to discover your significant tasks.

THE GREATEST GENERATION

Famed newscaster Tom Brokaw wrote an entire book about the group of people he termed the *Greatest Generation*. These are the people born in the 1920s and 1930s, who came of age during World War II. Brokaw considers them the Greatest Generation not only because of their service during wartime but because of the ways they changed the world forever.

When the war was over, the men and women who had been involved, in uniform and in civilian capacities, immediately began the task of rebuilding their lives and the world they wanted. They were mature beyond their years, tempered by what they had been through, disciplined by their military training and sacrifices. They married in record numbers and gave birth to another distinctive generation, the Baby Boomers. They stayed true to their values of personal responsibility, duty, honor, and faith.

They became part of the greatest investment in higher education that any society ever made, a generous tribute from a grateful nation . . . They left [college] campuses with degrees and a determination to make up for lost time. They were a new kind of army now, moving onto the landscapes of industry, science, art, public policy, all the fields of American life, bringing to them the same passions and discipline that had served them so well during the war.

They helped convert a wartime economy into the most powerful peacetime economy in history. They made breakthroughs in medicine and other sciences. They gave the world new art and literature. They came to understand the need for federal civil rights legislation. They gave America Medicare.

They helped rebuild the economies and political institutions of their former enemies . . . At every stage of their lives they were part of historic challenges and achievements of a magnitude the world had never before witnessed.[5]

The men and women who made up the Greatest Generation never considered themselves the center of the universe. Their rite of passage—we call it World War II—had taught them what it meant to sacrifice for a greater cause. Many among them had already given the ultimate sacrifice. Why was the Greatest Generation so great? They knew and embraced their significant tasks.

Designer Originals

When we help our children take on significant tasks, they have the freedom to find true contentment in who and what they are, in why they were created, and in what they were created to do. Now, not every child grows up to be a world leader, but every child can be a world *changer* by finding his appointed place in God's kingdom.

When you give your children tasks that gradually increase in significance, when you share with them about their importance and value to the family even when they are too young to understand completely, you are preparing them to accept God's bigger purposes for their lives.

"Yes," you will say, "this is your purpose right now: holding screwdrivers and carrying pitchers of grape Kool-Aid. But you won't be holding screwdrivers and carrying pitchers all your life! We're going to see all that God has for you today and tomorrow and the next day and the next."

This positive expectation helps kids think beyond themselves to God's plans—the ones he says are "good plans . . . not plans to hurt you" that will "give you hope and a good future" (Jer. 29:11 NCV). When you prepare your children to think and live in this way, you are putting back something that our culture has taken away.

Embracing the significant tasks that God brings into our lives helps us find out how the particular shape in which he created us fits his overall puzzle. After all, we know that he makes no mistakes. He knew us before we were born, and each one of us is "fearfully and wonderfully made" (Ps. 139:14 NKJV). Finding the significant tasks that he gives us helps us live peaceful, contented, abundant lives—the ones he created us to live.

One year, I traveled to Jerusalem to take a course at the Center for Biblical Studies. During my stay, I took time to visit a *kibbutz*, one of Israel's well-known communal farms. I saw how the people worked together to run the farm in cooperation. I saw the ladies cooking the communal meals together. Finally, they took me to their school.

I nearly laughed aloud. All of the children had their shirts on backward. Every shirt was buttoned down the back instead of the front. When I commented, the teachers told me proudly that these shirts were designer originals. They had been created that way intentionally. Every child needed another child to help him, and every child needed to help someone else.

I thought, *That's the way God created us. You need my significant tasks, and I need yours. God has intentionally created us this way. We're designer originals.*

⊰[RITE OF PASSAGE PARENTING SUMMARY]⊱

The agricultural-industrial cultural shift has removed the essential experience of significant tasks—special assignments that demonstrate an individual's worth to the people he considers important—from kids' lives. Until the cultural shift, young people were considered a capable, responsible part of society. They had important responsibilities and made valuable contributions to their families and to society.

Young people who don't have significant tasks—like the McDonald's Kids of today—look for pseudo-significant tasks that appear meaningful but have no lasting value. Taking on significant tasks gives parents and children alike the freedom to find contentment in who they are and what they have been created to do.

﹏

CHAPTER FIVE

How It Shows:
"You Can't Do That—
You're Just a Kid!"

The loss of significant tasks has left kids lacking in knowledge and skills for responsible living, and our culture prevents even kids who have these skills from performing significant tasks.

One of my students had an experience with an airline that clearly demonstrates the problems our culture has because of its shift away from giving significant tasks to emerging adults.

Fourteen-year-old Andrew Pieper had committed to giving up his spring break to serve others across the border in Mexico. The cross-cultural team to which we assigned him planned to minister to orphans living in children's homes. In order to raise money for this trip, Andrew acted as an adult. He printed and posted flyers offering his services as an amateur magician, cut and edged neighbors' lawns, and even spoke before a large group about his trip and the significant tasks he would assume during his week of service.

Andrew's trip was a significant task as well as a rite of passage event. On his own, he washed and folded his clothes, packed, and made sure he had everything he needed. The night before the trip, he spoke with his parents about the problems he might encounter, including missed connections or cancelled flights. He knew what to do in each situation. Andrew was all ready to go . . .

At least he and his parents thought so. Because of the extended period of adolescence that our society has created, we never assume that young people have the basic skills for living until they're much older than fourteen. Andrew had used the money he raised to pay an adult fare on a flight with a major airline. However, at the ticket counter, he discovered that, at least as far as the airline was concerned, he was just a kid.

Even though in only a few hours he would travel across the border and into another culture, taking on adult responsibilities and leaving his adolescence behind, the airline made him pay an "unaccompanied minor" fee of seventy-five dollars each way. As he boarded the plane, the airline required his dad to walk Andrew all the way through security and up to the door of the gate. When he had to change planes in another city, an airline attendant took him from the plane to a holding area and onto the next plane.

Our culture definitely sends mixed messages about significant tasks, just as it does about the age that adulthood begins. If a student like Andrew attempts to take on a significant task, society fights against him. At fourteen, Andrew was old enough to babysit his younger siblings, but the airline still said he needed a babysitter.

As he prepared for the trip and served in Mexico, Andrew acted as a McDavid's Teen, taking on adult responsibilities and significant tasks. Once he returned from Mexico and arrived at the airport, however, the airline once again told him he was only a McDonald's Kid, lacking in the knowledge and skills to understand posted departure times or find his way from one gate to another.

Is it any wonder our kids are having a hard time growing up? The few who dare to stand up and take on adult responsibilities find society standing right there to turn them away. A rite of passage event, which Andrew experienced in Mexico, clearly marks the line between childhood and adulthood. Our culture does its best to blur that distinction. Almost as soon as Andrew began taking on adult responsibilities and significant tasks, society said to him through the airline, "You can't do that—you're just a kid!"

JESUS' SIGNIFICANT TASK

As we have already seen, Jesus did not experience anything like Andrew's adventure. His family and his culture knew exactly when he became an adult. As a result, he did not experience the confusion of adolescence. In the temple in Jerusalem, Jesus demonstrated that he had experienced a rite of passage, but he also did something else. He was there to accomplish a significant task.

Jesus' time in the temple that day had a lasting impact on many lives. Had he not been there, he would not have been accomplishing God's will. In other words, if Jesus had not gone to the temple that day, he would have sinned.

Exactly why would it have been a sin for him to miss that temple appointment? Of course, Joseph, Mary, and Jesus went to Jerusalem "according to the custom of the feast" (Luke 2:42 NKJV). Until that year, Jesus, as a child, had not been required to attend. Now that he was a man, he was under a religious and cultural obligation to go—but would failing to meet that obligation have been a sin? Probably not.

When they found him in the temple, Jesus told his parents his true reason for being there: he was carrying out his heavenly Father's business (Luke 2:49). Scripture gives special emphasis to this temple event: it is the very first time Jesus testifies that he "does exactly what the Father [tells him] to do" (John 14:31 NCV). Jesus always did the things that were pleasing to his Father (John 8:29). This shows us that if he had *not* been there in the temple, he would have sinned.

If Jesus had sinned, he could not have been the perfect Savior God required for the redemption of mankind. The time he spent in the temple dialoguing with the lawyers was important preparation for what would be his most significant task: giving his life as an atoning sacrifice, and rising from the dead so we might have eternal life. This twelve-year-old boy had an incredible responsibility. If he had sinned by failing to obey his Father and follow him to the temple, the fate of the world would have entirely changed. Tasks don't get much more significant than that!

The Bible is filled with stories of people who fulfilled significant tasks assigned by God. If Noah had not accomplished his significant task, the entire world would have been sunk. People tried to tell David he was *just a kid*, too little to accomplish his first significant task, but he picked up five smooth stones and Goliath fell. Jonah sailed away from his significant task—and into the belly of a gigantic fish—but because he eventually accomplished it, an entire nation was saved.

Even if a significant task does not immediately appear important, eventually its value will show. However, we also need to look at the other side of this truth. Sooner or later, if you don't perform your significant task, other people will suffer. That's how we know Jesus' temple task was so significant.

JUNGLE SIGNIFICANCE

Over the last few years, I have come to know and love a group of people who understand the concept of significant task: the Choco tribe of Panama. One of the unique things about them is that every person, from the youngest to the oldest, has a significant task. The Choco carry their most elderly grandmother, a woman who can't even walk, to the center of the village every day in order to allow her to carry out her significant task: keeping the communal fire going. She holds a huge leaf that she waves to fan the flames and keep the embers hot. Occasionally, she reaches into the fire with a stick, stirring it around to keep the coals burning. Everyone in the Choco tribe depends on this grandmother to have the fire ready, even though she is the weakest and oldest person among them.

This is a strong contrast to our culture, in which the weakest, oldest people often wind up in nursing homes, where they have very few significant tasks. And what do the people who live in nursing homes talk about? The good old days—when they all had significant tasks.

Not only does every member of the Choco tribe have significant tasks, but the Choco give their visitors significant tasks too. Each significant task fits into the bigger picture of the tribal work. When we stay with this people group, some of our students get the job of going into the jungle and gathering leaves. Now, these leaves are not your mother's geranium leaves. In fact, they are big enough to swallow your mother whole.

Gathering the leaves and carrying them through the jungle to the village (where the tribe uses them to make roofs for their homes) is challenging, to say the least. I know about this job because it was my first significant task with the Choco.

Others that they have assigned us include fishing and debarking trees by beating them with a stick.

Don't ask me how, but on a recent trip there, I pulled the night shift. After a long, hard day in the jungle, I tend to be pretty tired, so I was less than excited about having to go out after dark—even for a significant task. In the first place, I showed up in my white T-shirt. The Choco people sent me back to my sleeping area for a black shirt. I couldn't believe it. Here I was, deep in the jungles of Panama, admonished for failing to comply with the dress code.

My Choco partners each had a spear, but they gave me a ball-pen hammer. They explained that their job (significant task) was to catch the crocodile. Mine was to use the hammer to make sure this reptile reached his eternal destiny as quickly as possible.

The Choco hunters tie ropes to the barbs of their spears. When the spear connects with the flesh of its victim, the rope pulls the stick handle back and the barb goes forward. It's a great system, and since I had to go crocodile hunting dressed in black while floating down a jungle river with my Choco friends in the middle of the night, I was eager to see it work.

The Choco have this adventure down to a science. First, they float down the river in a boat carved from a log. One hunter stands frozen at the bow of the boat, spear at the ready. The other stands frozen at the stern, also with a spear. Me? That night, I was also in position, hammer and black T-shirt in place, right in the middle of the log boat. I began to wonder if the Choco crocodile hunters had heard the phrase "eliminate the middleman."

My tribal buddies explained to me that the crocodiles would not move out of reach because they mistake the logs floating down the river for logs. Sure enough, the man in front spotted a crocodile almost immediately. It didn't move out of the way, so he stabbed it with his spear.

Suddenly, everything exploded. The crocodile went into defense mode and began spinning in the water. The guy in the prow of the boat, still holding the rope tied to the barb of the spear, knew well that the crocodile could easily pull him off the boat and into the river. He held the rope tightly as the crocodile continued its death roll, wrapping the rope more and more tightly around itself. Together, he and the other Choco hunter picked up the furious reptile and put him right where I didn't want him . . . the bottom of the boat.

Again, as the middleman, my job was to use the ball-pen hammer to knock the crocodile on the soft spot right in the middle of his forehead, and I was ready for my significant task. However, I never got to experience it. Choco custom dictates that crocodiles must be at least seven feet long before the tribe kills them for food, and that night, none of the crocodiles met the requirement. The hunters knew without even measuring that the crocodiles were too short, so they made the decision to send them back over the side of the boat.

That whole experience is why I feel justified in telling people that I'm a crocodile hunter. The only problem is that I've never killed a crocodile. I have met several, however . . . up close and personal.

The Choco people do not concern themselves with happiness or personal fulfillment. They are equally unconcerned with how old or young the fire-stirrers or the leaf-stackers or the bark-strippers or even the crocodile hunters are. They know that they have the skills for survival as individuals and as a culture.

Just as people in our culture did before the shift, the Choco people know who they are because of what they do. "I'm a fire-stirrer." "I'm a leaf-stacker." "I'm a bark-stripper."

And even, "I'm a crocodile hunter." They know who they are and what they can do because each has a significant task.

How It Shows

Our culture and the Choco culture are very different—and not just because we don't generally float down the river to hunt crocodiles. When our culture shifted and we lost the concept of significant tasks, we also lost the concept of gradually building skills for responsible living into our children's lives. This has left our kids lacking the ability to take on significant tasks at an appropriate time. It's hard to be self-reliant if no one has trained you the way John Sr. and Grandpa Walton trained John-Boy.

> In the smaller, more stable rural settings, children were offered opportunities to learn life skills through on-the-job training because they were needed to help the family function and survive. On the other hand, in the new urban/suburban setting, children did not have real opportunities to learn the skills they needed to become capable adults. They were not needed in the day-to-day functioning of families. They frequently spent a large portion of their time watching television, which included a variety of programs and concepts that were counter-productive to the development of skills and capabilities for successful living.
>
> Today, increasing numbers of children have fewer and fewer opportunities to experience a meaningful role in family life and social institutions. Without a mean-ingful role, it is difficult to develop a sense of meaning, purpose, and significance through being needed, lis-tened to, and taken seriously.[1]

We have exactly the opposite situation that the Choco have: we *don't* know who we are, because we don't know what we can do. This may explain the large number of students who push adult responsibilities farther away by spending extra years in college and graduate school. Even that extended education, however, is no guarantee of readiness for life as a capable, responsible adult.

> As Tracy, mother of [twentysomething] Jed, said, "He's got one foot in the adult world and the other foot in the sandbox." . . . Christine, a 53-year-old insurance agent, said, "My son, Evan, is larger than life and confident that he can do anything. In fact, he runs political campaigns and can pick up the phone and call corporate executives and local politicians. Yet, he isn't comfortable opening up a checking account without my assistance."[2]

Growing up in an agricultural society helps you move toward adult responsibilities from the moment you are born. You work in the field. You churn the butter. You wash the clothes. You prepare meals. You don't have time or energy to think about what you can't do, or what someone else should do for you.

When I was growing up, I knew that my family valued me because I contributed to our family's success through my chores and other jobs. I knew that I was needed.

The Need to Be Needed

Educator Stephen Glenn reminds us that all people have a well-defined "need to be needed" that is often stronger than the need to survive.[3] When Caleb asked to help fix the car and tried to carry the grape Kool-Aid, he was showing his need to be needed. He wanted to have a place of value and worth in his family. When we fail to give our children significant tasks, this need goes unmet.

However, as Glenn notes, children are not the only ones who need to be needed. As he points out, research shows that adults who view themselves as fulfilling an important role in society produce more, experience better health, and recover from illness more quickly than those who believe their work is insignificant or unimportant. In other words, if you consider yourself a leftover, it's easy to believe that life is not worth living.[4]

Significant tasks define your value and worth to society. Little Johnny and his friends from the '60s filled their lives with pseudo-significant tasks because God created them with a deep-seated need to be needed. The little girl who wants to help mommy cook and the little boy who wants to help daddy mow the lawn share that same need.

When he was only about ten years old, my son Jeremiah understood the need to be needed better than many of today's kids. One January day, he came home from school without his coat. I noticed the problem and immediately switched into frustrated-father mode: "Where's your coat? Did you leave it at school? It's *cold* outside."

Once he could get a word in edgewise, Jeremiah explained. "Dad, there's a boy at school. He doesn't have a coat—not even a jacket. I knew I had some other coats at home, so I thought it would be okay to give him that one."

I had nothing else to say. How could I? Once again, Jeremiah had exactly the right answer. He had decided, without any input from Cathy or me, to take care of his friend by giving him not just any coat but his very *best* one. Oklahoma winters are cold, and Jeremiah recognized the need. He could fulfill that need and feel good about himself in the process. Jeremiah had found a significant task.

Techno-Significance

When kids lack significant tasks, they make up their own. However, pseudo-significant tasks today look very different from those Little Johnny and his '60s friends invented. Today's kids perform multiple pseudo-significant tasks, as an article in *Time* relates, all at the same time. "There is no doubt that the [multitasking] phenomenon has reached a kind of warp speed in the era of Web-enabled computers, when it has become routine to conduct six IM conversations, watch *American Idol* on TV, and Google the names of last season's finalists all at once."[5]

Kids spend hours on the cell phone and computer, text-messaging or IM-ing, fueled by the need to feel needed—for someone to know (and care) that they exist. They spend hours talking to strangers online. They put up weblogs on Xanga or MySpace, posting their thoughts so others can read and respond. Multiple times a day, they seek affirmation, value, and meaning through technology by means of these electronic pseudo-significant tasks. Like Little Johnny and his friends, they are propping up their self-esteem with false fronts, still searching for something truly significant.

Outsourced

The problems caused by the loss of significant tasks show up in the lives of parents too. As we switched from an agricultural to an industrial society, many basic survival skills began to erode. We no longer plant and grow food for our families. Instead, we drive down to the local grocery supercenter, depending on Libby's to put the vegetables on our table and on Ragu to make our spaghetti sauce. We trust Braum's or United Dairy Farmers to provide our milk. If we want a snack, we even depend on our friend Orville Redenbacher to put butter, salt, and popcorn in a special bag.

Since our culture has moved to the suburbs, we no longer have room to plant corn or a place to pasture a cow. We have to trust others to provide the things we used to take care of ourselves. Since we don't have the skills to do the things that used to be significant tasks, we outsource them.

Many people today take things a step further and outsource their cooking altogether. Americans spend more than a billion dollars a day dining out.[6] Even if we don't eat out, some of us hire a personal chef, a growing trend in our culture, when the significant task of preparing meals grows inconvenient. When we do manage to cook, we typically use a large number of prepared foods. Before the cultural shift, there was no such thing, for example, as Hamburger Helper. The only *hamburger helper* was mom or sister or whoever took on the significant task of preparing dinner. Meal preparation has been outsourced.

We also outsource our children's education. We no longer consider it our responsibility to ensure that our children gain the skills and knowledge for living. Instead, we outsource education to the schools. After all, it's their job to make our kids smart . . . and if our kids don't perform well on standardized tests or get into the right colleges, we march right up to the campus and complain. Now that the culture has shifted, we hold others accountable for the significant tasks that used to be ours. Naturally, since we hold the schools responsible for educating our kids, we follow them to college and beyond to make sure the job is done right.

> Parents have so assumed the right to take every step of college orientation with their kids that the University of Vermont is hiring and rigorously training selected senior students as "parent bouncers." Their job is to keep the adults from orientation sessions in which their incoming offspring consult with academic advisors or participate in peer discussions about alcohol and sex.[7]

Our children's education has been outsourced.

We also outsource our family's entertainment. That significant task now belongs not to the mother or brother who played the piano while the family sang songs together or to the father who told stories around the fire but to MTV, Disney, PlayStation, and Nintendo. When it comes to entertainment, everything's outsourced.

⌒

WE'VE TAUGHT OUR CHILDREN THAT WHEN YOU HAVE A SIGNIFICANT TASK, YOU DON'T DO IT YOURSELF. INSTEAD, YOU PAY SOMEONE ELSE TO TAKE CARE OF IT FOR YOU.

Our culture also outsources its spiritual development. We hire the youth minister to take care of our kids' spiritual lives. Naturally, if we don't think they're getting what they need, we call him up and complain, or we change churches. The spiritual development of our families has been outsourced.

Someday in the future, when we become old and weak, we should not be surprised when our kids fail to take responsibility for our care. After all, we've taught them that when you have a significant task, you don't do it yourself. Instead, you pay someone else to take care of it for you. Since we haven't trained our children in responsible living, we shouldn't be a bit surprised when *we're* outsourced.

God designed significant tasks to teach us to take responsibility for our own lives. Those who perform them become capable, responsible, and self-reliant. Our culture shows its lack of significant tasks when it produces adults who lack these qualities.

Every generation has the job of equipping its children for their significant tasks. Right now, in fact, we have an entire generation that's not very well equipped for the significant task of raising capable young people. Since we don't have the skills to do it, even the parenting job has been outsourced. *Rite of Passage Parenting* aims to break that cycle, returning a sense of freedom and responsibility to parents who practice it.

After all, I know you're a good parent! You want your kids to have good things to eat. You want them to receive a great education. You want them to have fun. You want them to embrace spiritual truths and go to church regularly. That's why you take time and energy to check up on the college professor, or fifth-grade teacher, or Little League coach, or youth minister.

Rite of Passage Parenting wants to help you take a step backward and look at your own responsibilities in these areas. You may even find that when you begin leading your children into their significant tasks, you will discover your own.

∘{ Rite of Passage Parenting Summary }∘

Our culture tells young people that they cannot take on a rite of passage or significant tasks. Jesus not only experienced a rite of passage at the temple in Jerusalem, he also performed a significant task. Significant tasks help establish your identity because what you *do* defines who you *are*. God has created each of us with the need to be needed—the desire for a significant task.

Because of the agricultural-industrial cultural shift, parents have outsourced many aspects of childrearing. By doing so, we have indirectly taught kids that you don't have to take on significant tasks—you hire others to perform them for you. The loss of significant tasks has left many young adults lacking in knowledge and skills for living. Society tells even those who have these skills, "You can't do that—you're just a kid!"

CHAPTER SIX

ESSENTIAL EXPERIENCE #2: EXTEND THEIR LIFE SKILLS THROUGH SIGNIFICANT TASKS

We can help our kids move toward adulthood in a healthy way by assigning sequential developmental tasks that move them toward significant tasks.

A parent who gives a child significant tasks gains freedom. God designed the parenting process this way. He intends that you move your child from infancy (totally dependent) to adulthood (capable, responsible, and self-reliant). As kids take on significant tasks, parents are gradually released from responsibility for their care. Knowing that you have prepared your children through Rite of Passage Parenting will give you tremendous peace of mind. That's freedom!

When my boys were growing up, I started thinking about specific ways to move them toward capable, responsible adulthood. Although we no longer lived in an agricultural society, Cathy and I still needed to equip them for life by helping them grow in knowledge and skills. But how?

The answer, of course, was to give them significant tasks; specifically, tasks that related to the needs of *our* family in *our* culture. Cathy and I looked at our adult responsibilities, and the first one we thought of was something every parent understands: paying the bills.

We decided that paying one of our monthly bills would make a good start for Jeremiah, then nine years old. It became his job to pay the electric bill. Of course, even as levelheaded as Jeremiah is, he wasn't born knowing how to pay bills. We had to teach him.

Once we had gone through the training process, which I'll describe later, Jeremiah watched for that electric bill every month. Because of this significant task, he quickly learned what it costs to run a household. He knew his job was important. After all, we had told him that if he failed to pay the bill, he would have to take money from his allowance and have the electricity turned back on.

Not long after Jeremiah had assumed this first significant task, we had a family meeting. I had just come back from teaching a youth camp, excited because I had earned an extra three hundred dollars. For a youth minister, that's like hitting the lottery. During our meeting, our family discussed what to do with this financial windfall.

I had my presentation ready. I just *knew* we should buy a video camera. I could easily justify the expense. After all, we would use the camera to film our children's upbringing, documenting all their important activities and preserving family memories. I finished my little speech, leaned back in my chair, and looked around, waiting for the approving comments of my wife and sons.

Somehow, those comments never came ... but Jeremiah spoke up right away. "Dad, we have a big electric bill this month— and you want to spend three hundred dollars on a *camera*? You know we don't really need that—but we *have* to pay our electric bill."

Even at nine years old, Jeremiah was already thinking like

an adult; he knew that taking care of *wants* before *needs* wasn't right for our family—or any family. You probably won't be surprised to learn that when Jeremiah graduated from college years later, he did something many students fail to do: Jeremiah graduated debt-free.

Faithful in Little; Faithful in Much

When kids are not given significant tasks, they don't learn the skills that make them capable, responsible adults. But by allowing them to grow in skills and knowledge, we encourage them to gradually increase their level of responsibility.

Jesus taught this principle through the parable of the talents in Matthew 25:14–30. A master leaves on a journey and gives three of his slaves differing amounts of talents (money). The first and second slaves invest their portions and bring back double the amount they originally received. The third slave is too afraid to do anything, so he buries the money.

The master tells each of the slaves who doubled his investment, "Well done, good and faithful servant; you were faithful over a few things, I will make you ruler over many things. Enter into the joy of your lord" (Matt. 25:21, 23 NKJV). When he entrusted them with the money, the master was giving his slaves tasks that were designed to move them toward significant tasks. Because they were faithful with "a few things" today, their master would entrust them with "many things" tomorrow.

Simulator Tasks

As I studied the ways to "fix it, brother!" for this generation, I realized that we have skipped an important step in training our children. The chores my parents gave me as a kid were smaller significant tasks that prepared me for greater ones. Kids today don't usually get that kind of training. They haven't proven that they're faithful in little, so they're not ready to be entrusted with much.

> ⟿ SIMULATOR TASKS: Sequential, developmental activities that build skills for living and prepare the one who performs them for significant tasks.

I have coined a term that describes this necessary and gradual preparation very well: *simulator tasks*. These are the activities that build the skills for performing significant tasks. I have a friend who trains commercial pilots, and he tells me that all of them must receive training in a simulator, where they spend hours going through every worst-case scenario possible.

RITE OF PASSAGE
SIMULATOR AND SIGNIFICANT TASKS

Through simulator and significant tasks, a child learns the skills to become a capable and self-reliant adult.

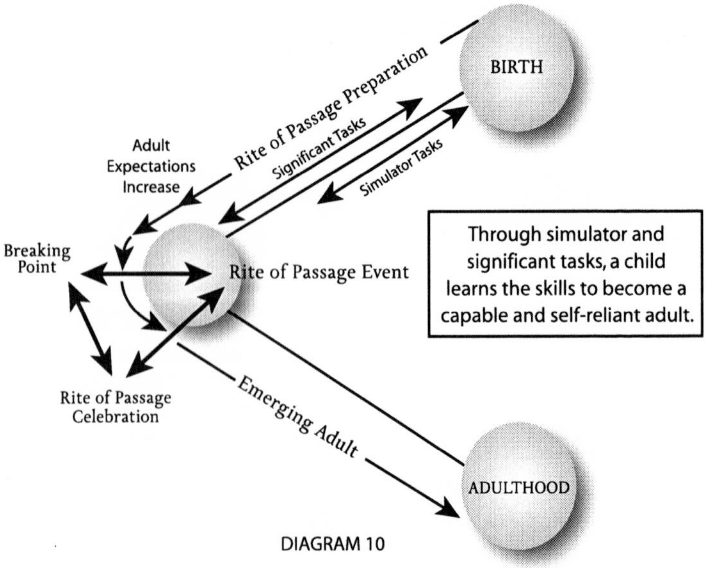

DIAGRAM 10

Airlines require their pilots to do simulator training because they want them ready to respond in an emergency. Even pilots who have flown for years must return to the simulator periodically to sharpen their skills. After all, many people are relying on the competence and capability of their pilot, who sits at the controls of a ninety-ton projectile hurtling through the air at seven hundred miles per hour. Because of their training, when the pilots are in the real aircraft with real passengers, they have the ability to handle any circumstance or situation thrown their way.

Driven to Distraction

Simulator tasks cannot, however, take the place of real-life experience. I learned this when I made the nearly fatal mistake of trying to teach my oldest son to drive. I should have figured it out when Jeremiah told me that he was ready to drive because he had completed an entire *semester* of driver's education. In fact, he implied, I had nothing left to teach him.

When I was growing up, everybody learned to drive on farm equipment. I remember driving when my feet could barely touch the pedals of my dad's tractor, which had a top speed of two miles per hour. If something went wrong, you had at least forty acres to correct it.

Sure that I had more to share with Jeremiah about the manly art of driving, I got into the car and began to expound on the tremendous responsibility he was now assuming. Interrupting my speech, my son informed me that if your car was traveling at sixty miles per hour and you slammed on your brakes, you would cause your passengers to experience three g's of force.

In all my years of watching *Jeopardy*, I have never seen that category. "Yes, Alex. Car g-forces for $200." I have been driving for over thirty years and have done very well without that kind of information. Sure, Jeremiah may know the car's g-forces, but can anyone teach him to figure out how many miles it gets to a gallon of gas?

With motor on, transmission engaged, and foot to the accelerator, we began the driving lesson. I found myself repeatedly urging my son to "Watch it, watch *it*. Watch it! You are too close to the shoulder!"

"That's the way we learned to drive at school," he replied.

Never had I experienced the fear of God more than when Jeremiah began accelerating down the road. As I sat helplessly strapped in beside him, I had never prayed harder for Jesus to return . . . right away!

After he ran the wheels up over a curb and continued down the road, weaving from side to side, I asked him if this was also the way he drove at school. At this point, he informed me that nearly all of his driving time had taken place in a simulator. "But, Dad . . . I did a *lot* of time in the simulator. It's just like the real thing."

When we finally reached home, I immediately resigned my position as driving instructor. I had lasted all of twenty-three minutes.

Although Jeremiah eventually learned to drive, he did not learn from me. His mother taught him. I decided that anyone who had survived childbirth would find teaching a teenager to drive a piece of cake.

DESIRE: A FIRM FOUNDATION

Because Jeremiah had experience in the driving simulator, he thought he had already learned everything he needed to know. Instead, he had to move from the simulator into real driving by completing certain tasks. In the same way, our kids need to move from simulator tasks into significant tasks through some very specific steps. Rite of Passage Parents can build both *simulator* and *significant* tasks into kids' lives on a similar solid foundation—not of skill or knowledge, but *desire*. This genuine longing to help and contribute to the family prepares kids to take on tasks that increase in responsibility. We want to cultivate in our children the desire to be faithful in little things so that later we can trust them with much.

As a boy I lived outside of Buckner, Missouri—a small, rural community east of Kansas City. I attended a tiny country church called Six Mile Baptist. I know you have seen churches like it—those little white-framed buildings with the cemetery in the back.

Looking back, I have tried to understand why I have such pleasant memories of those days, and simulator tasks play a large part. I remember when the church needed to build an educational wing; as the men of Six Mile Baptist gathered to raise the building, we boys worked alongside them. I swept the floors, pushed wheelbarrow-loads of cement, and helped pull electrical wires.

A boy gains a certain satisfaction when he does a man's job. I remember dragging my little body home every evening, thinking that I couldn't move another step. Of course, this lasted until my brother asked if I wanted to play baseball, when the tiredness vanished immediately.

Although pushing the wheelbarrow and pulling the electrical wires were not true significant tasks, they were simulator tasks: these tasks, combined with the encouragement of the men, prepared me—both in terms of skills and desire—to assume greater tasks as I matured. Through these simulator tasks, I was given an opportunity to show myself faithful in little so that, as I grew in skills and knowledge, I could become faithful in much.

As our young people engage in simulator tasks, we must remember to encourage them, as the men of Six Mile Baptist encouraged me. This will cultivate in these emerging adults the desire they need to take on even more significant tasks and become fully capable, responsible adults. Affirming our children's individual worth and the value of the contributions they make *today* builds their desire to take on significant tasks *tomorrow*.

When Caleb held the screwdriver as I attempted to work on the car, he was performing a simulator task. Earlier, I referred to it as a significant task—and that's how Caleb perceived it at four years old. Today, as a young adult, he would help me with this same job, but he would certainly not perceive it as a significant task.

Rite of Passage Parents will give their kids simulator tasks that build in them, from a very young age, their desire to ask, "Can I help?" If you fail to do this, you will find it a challenge to produce that same desire in their hearts at age thirteen when you suddenly assign significant tasks. Although they may be old enough to take on these tasks, they will lack the desire to do so. Beyond that, if you haven't developed their skills and knowledge through simulator tasks they won't know how.

SLOWLY, SLOWLY GROWS THE ELEPHANT

Before he began his teaching career, my college Greek professor spent years working with tribal groups in Africa. When we would express frustration with some aspect of our language learning, he would always quote the same Swahili

proverb, "Slowly, slowly grows the elephant." He used this saying to tell us that neither elephants, nor Rome, nor the knowledge of Greek is built in a day. He helped us to build our
command of the language little by little and step-by-step.

In the same way, we build simulator tasks on top of simulator tasks into our kids' lives, properly laying the foundation
for future significant tasks. This is a part of the rite of passage preparation discussed earlier in the book in chapter 3.

An agricultural society provides a systematic way of doing
this. You don't butcher the cows when you are three years old.
Instead, you start out by herding them and carrying their feed.
The culture allows for this natural progression from smaller
simulator tasks to larger ones and, eventually, to significant tasks.

In my job, I travel and speak to many people, including groups
of college students. I have talked with a number of resident advi-
sors (RAs)—upperclassmen who supervise younger students
living in dormitories—who tell me about the problems they
face because students lack basic skills for living. One young
woman, her RA told me, packed a dormitory washing machine
so full of dirty clothes that its agitator could not even spin. She
had never done a load of wash before.

Rite of Passage Parenting emphasizes that *slowly, slowly,*
you need to give your kids simulator tasks that build skills
and responsibility. For example, I recommend that you teach
your kids to do their own laundry by the age of eight. It costs
only about twenty-five cents to do a load of wash. You can give
your child valuable skills for living that many others lack a
quarter at a time.

We've all seen mother birds patiently teaching their babies
to fly. In our day, we follow the opposite pattern. At a certain
point, we kick our children out of the nest and expect them to
fly—*without any simulator training*. We haven't taken the time to

build significant tasks into their lives. Since our overgrown baby birds have spent no time on simulator tasks, they have no skills for living. Small wonder that many end up as Boomerang or B2B kids.

Remember, mom and dad, it's never too late. If you have older kids who haven't learned to perform the tasks they need to take care of themselves, you can start today. That way, they won't remain stuck in the simulator, but will move on confidently to increasingly significant tasks. They will have the skills to handle their lives as capable, responsible, self-reliant adults.

STEPS TO SIGNIFICANCE

Jesus modeled the sequential steps of simulator tasks perfectly as he moved his disciples toward significant tasks. You'll remember their statement, "Lord, teach us to pray" (Luke 11:1 NCV).

Why do you think his disciples asked him to teach them to pray? They recognized his connection with God as an important part of his life—they could see it was significant to *him*. Often they arrived in a place and had trouble finding their Master. Every time, he was out praying. They also noticed that whatever he prayed for, happened.

Jesus wanted to emulate his heavenly Father. As he did this, the disciples watched their Master and wanted to be like him. As he began equipping them to pray, he told them he was modeling his life after his Father's: "But Jesus said, 'I tell you the truth, the Son can do nothing alone. The Son does only what he sees the Father doing, because the Son does whatever the Father does'" (John 5:19 NCV).

First, Jesus *modeled* prayer for his disciples, doing exactly as the Father had taught him, and they watched with interest.

Then, he began to *instruct* them with the knowledge and skills they needed. Next, he prayed *alongside* them so that they could watch and understand his teaching. Finally, he sent them out to pray *on their own* as he watched. At first, they didn't do very well; in fact, they kept falling asleep. Later, they seemed to get the hang of it. Some of them wrote his instructions for prayer down in the book we call the New Testament.

ALL WASHED UP

Teaching eight-year-olds to do the laundry? Teaching a nine-year-old to pay the electric bill? How does Rite of Passage Parenting accomplish this? I think you know the answer, because you're a good parent. The ability to perform these tasks does not come overnight—you develop it in your child "slowly, slowly," through the wise use of smaller simulator tasks. Then, you follow Jesus' example of modeling, taking a child all the way through the steps he or she is to follow.

When kids are learning to read, we don't hand them the encyclopedia and ask them to check out the article on Outer Mongolia. Instead, we begin with the basics: letters, sounds, blends, small words, bigger words, and sentences—slowly, slowly. Before we know it, they're stumbling through their first easy reader, and it's not long before they can tackle chapter books.

When you teach your kids simulator tasks, take that same approach. First, *model the task*: you demonstrate the task as they watch. Remember to encourage and affirm your children as you move through the process. This helps retain the "Can I help?" desire.

Next, move to the step of *instruction*. Teach them about the task and the equipment or supplies involved. Show them what you expect them to accomplish, demonstrating the *process* (for example, straightening and dusting the room; running the washer) along with the *product* (an orderly room; clean clothes). In this way, you are giving them the knowledge and skills they need and helping them gain confidence for future tasks.

Move to the next step: have them *perform the task alongside you* only when they have practiced the basics and seem to understand them. Like Jesus' disciples, they are not ready to be left alone quite yet, and having you there builds their confidence. You may want to take on the role of the helper—and your kids will enjoy telling you what to do. When they make a mistake, assume the problem was with your instruction rather than their attention and correct them gently. At this point, you may even want to have them help you write out a simple chart, specific for this task, to help remind them what to do.

Finally, your kids can *perform the simulator task on their own.* Like the disciples, they may make mistakes, but by now, they have been helping you with the task for some time. They are ready for the challenge and will take pride in their ability to accomplish it alone.

At a recent conference, a couple came up to me with their eight-year-old son. He wanted to thank me for encouraging them to teach him to take responsibility for his laundry. He was proud to tell me that he sorted, washed, dried, and folded all of his own clothes, something few of today's McDonald's Kids accomplish. Doing his own laundry was helping this young man grow up.

What You Don't Inspect, They Don't Expect

I want to stop here and explain a principle that applies to all simulator tasks. Even after you have finished the step-by-step process explained above, go back and inspect your kids' work. They need to know that you care enough about their efforts to check to make sure they've done things properly. I like to say, *What you don't inspect, they don't expect.*

Do not allow yourself to be tempted into skipping the element of inspection. After all, if you tell me to clean up my room and then never come back to look at it, my spirit says, "They don't really care anyway." When you're training students in simulator tasks, the inspection time is the place where you do gentle correcting when misunderstandings or mistakes have occurred. Your inspection of my simulator task means that you value my time and my work.

CHECKING OUT

We can apply the same steps Jesus used, with minor adaptations, to almost any simulator task we need to teach our kids. In fact, I recommend applying those same steps to significant tasks. Let's look at Jeremiah's bill-paying experience again.

[Note: Jeremiah learned to pay the electric bill by using a checkbook, but many people pay bills online. The process for online banking is very similar to what we used, substituting the computer, mouse, and Web site for the checkbook, pen, and stamped envelope. A child can acquire either or both of these skills as a simulator task, leading to the significant task of paying the bill independently.]

MODELING:

First, Cathy and I modeled paying the electric bill with Jeremiah watching. Since most kids do not know what a *bill* is, we helped him make the connection between the electric meter and the piece of paper that came in the mail. We showed him the meter's spinning needle and explained that the amount owed each month depended on how much electricity we used. We told Jeremiah that since we did not want to pay more money than necessary, we turned the lights off when we left a room. We even told him that the dollars we saved on our electric bill by being careful could go toward other items our family needed or wanted.

We also told him how important it was that he paid the bill each month: if we missed a payment, our lights would go off, and we would not be able to watch television or listen to music. We built the desire in his heart to assume this simulator task by showing him its true importance. By the time we had thoroughly modeled the task, Jeremiah knew it was essential, and he wanted to help.

INSTRUCTION:

Next, we showed Jeremiah the supplies he needed to pay the electric bill (bill, checkbook, pen, stamp) and talked about what we did when we wrote a check. First, we had to explain the concept of a checking account. We explained that the bank has an important rule: you must make more deposits than withdrawals. We showed him where to find the balance in the checkbook register, and how to subtract from it the amount of the check.

Next, we instructed him in the exact way to pay the bill. He watched as we removed the bill from the envelope, determined the amount due, wrote the check (correctly filling in all the blanks), signed it, and then subtracted its amount in the register. We explained each part of the process. Finally, we showed him how to fill out and tear off the bill stub; put it with the check into the envelope; seal, stamp, and mail the bill. Jeremiah had seen it all.

PERFORM WITH YOU ALONGSIDE:

After a couple of months of instruction, Jeremiah was ready to pay the bill with Cathy and me at his side. He was confident because he had been watching us carefully and listening to what we told him. We praised his successes and gently corrected any mistakes as he worked through the process. He had to show us that he could correctly perform each step except signing the check, which we did after he filled it out and presented it to us.

PERFORM ON HIS OWN:

Finally, Jeremiah no longer needed modeling or instruction, although we would have gone back to those stages if we had seen any problem areas. At the age of nine, he was completely in charge of the electric bill—and he did a great job. He had prepared to take on this significant task through simulator tasks that built skills for living into his life. Later, he would apply these skills to other areas of his life through a process that psychologists call *transference of learning.* This means that Jeremiah was learning more than just how to pay the electric bill. We were equipping him for life.

MATCH POINT

After Christmas one year, my mom, Lucile (you'll read more about her later), came home with a story. She had gone to visit her extended family, including Gordon, a relative by marriage, who grew up in South Africa.

On Christmas morning, the family gathered around the fireplace to read the biblical account of Christ's birth. Gordon volunteered to build the fire. Lucile watched as he came in with a load of wood and began stacking it in a unique way. She said it reminded her of the fires in the old Oklahoma cowboy camps. The wood was stacked teepee fashion and purposefully placed to burn thoroughly—and it did, throughout the family celebration.

Later in the day, Lucile asked Gordon where he had learned to build such an amazing fire. He explained that in his South African community, all the boys learn to build fires this way. Women do the inside cooking, but men fix the meat outside. At four years of age, boys are taught to gather the wood, learning to choose the types and sizes that will produce the best fire. The boys do not progress beyond wood gathering until age six, when they learn to stack the wood in the teepee style that Lucile had observed. They are taught to place it so that the air can reach each piece, so the fire continues to burn.

Finally, when the boys in this community turn eight years old, they receive a special gift: the match that allows them to light a fire for the first time. Every boy from eight years old and up has all the knowledge and skills he needs to build and light a fire, so he can cook the meat for the family. You guessed it: for the young men of this South African community, fire building is a significant task.

⊰[RITE OF PASSAGE PARENTING SUMMARY]⊱

We equip our kids with skills and knowledge by assigning *simulator tasks* that build sequentially and prepare them for significant tasks. As they prove their faithfulness to carry out small responsibilities, we can entrust them with greater ones. We also need to build their desire to help by encouraging and affirming them as they complete these simulator tasks.

We can follow Jesus' example with his disciples by taking our children through the steps: modeling the task, giving instruction about each step of the task, having the learner perform alongside us, and allowing the learner to perform the task on his or her own. In this way our children develop the skills they need to attain capable, responsible, self-reliant adulthood.

LOGICAL CONSEQUENCES

〜

CHAPTER SEVEN

WHAT'S MISSING:
KIDS NEED LOGICAL
CONSEQUENCES

The shifting culture has removed logical consequences—
predictable outcomes of an action—from our kids' lives.

O ne morning while Cathy was out running errands, I received a call from the principal of Caleb's school. "Mr. Moore, I just wanted you to know that your son forgot to bring his lunch today. I need you to go home, pick it up, and bring it to school right away."

I recognized this moment as an opportunity to work together with the school administration. We could combine our forces to teach Caleb another lesson in logical consequences. I began to tell the principal about our family's practice. Because Caleb already knew that he was responsible to take his own lunch to school, he would *never expect* me to leave my job, drive seven miles to my house, pick up his lunch, drive three miles to school, and then make the trip back to my office. Caleb understood that if he forgot his lunch, he would have to work things out himself.

I wasn't concerned about my creative son missing a meal.

After all, how hard would getting an extra sandwich or bag of chips be for a kid who could convince the school nurse that he had diabetes? As I began to explain our use of logical consequences, I told the principal, "I know Caleb won't starve. Today, he will probably have the best school lunch he's ever had. He will wheel and deal and do *something* to solve his problem."

I was ready to tell the principal some other alternatives that would provide logical consequences, such as allowing Caleb to work off the price of his lunch by sweeping floors or cleaning chalkboards, but he was a busy man, and he cut short my explanations. "Sir, we just can't do that. I'm sorry you feel this way." Abruptly, he hung up the phone.

I wasn't sure what the principal planned to do with the information I had given him, and I promptly did what dads seem to do on a regular basis: I forgot all about Caleb and his missing lunch. The principal never called back, and Caleb never told us about what had happened. It was almost as though the forgotten lunch and the principal's phone call had never happened.

Until three days later. That afternoon, an envelope from the school district appeared in the mailbox, addressed to me. Mildly curious, I opened it to find the principal's solution for Caleb's problem: a bill for one hot lunch.

Even at a young age, Caleb knew and understood all about logical consequences. He had regularly experienced them in our home: If you work hard in school, you will make good grades. If you don't get up in time, you will miss breakfast. If you don't get your homework done, you will miss watching your favorite television show. Each of these represents an action and its predictable outcome, or logical consequence.

Because of our family's regular use of logical consequences, I had no doubt that on the strength of just *one* missed meal,

Caleb would remember his lunch for a number of days in a row. The school officials, as representatives of our society, had a completely different idea. They believed that Caleb should not experience the logical consequences of failing to bring his lunch. They believed that I as a parent should step in and experience those logical consequences on my son's behalf. I should sacrifice by taking time from my work to make the ten-mile drive to deliver his lunch—or pay the price via a bill sent to my home. That day, the school district indirectly said to Caleb, "If you forget your lunch and your parents don't bail you out, the government will."

⊷ Logical Consequences: The predictable outcomes of an action.

What's Missing

Our society teaches this same lesson at various levels. No longer do we follow the advice of the apostle Paul, "If anyone will not work, neither shall he eat" (2 Thess. 3:10 NKJV). This is a great example of logical consequences—something that is becoming increasingly rare in our society. All too often, we take the *logic* out of logical consequences so that our kids rarely experience predictable outcomes of any kind. We place such an emphasis on building kids' self-esteem that we reward them for the smallest of right actions . . . and sometimes even for wrong ones. Columnist and author Betsy Hart shares two such examples from a principal of a Chicago parochial school.

In the first example, the principal says that when a child receives detention for being tardy, parents often ask to serve the detention in his place, even if the tardiness was solely the fault of the child. Parents who do this effectively shield their children from the logical consequences of tardiness.

The second example involves a four-year-old who took an earring from a department store without paying for it. After helping her child return the stolen goods, the mother then took her little girl to a toy store to select a surprise.[1]

Is receiving a treat a logical consequence for stealing? Of course not! Although the mother of the four-year-old almost certainly did not realize it, she not only caused her daughter to miss the logical consequences for stealing, but she replaced those consequences with a reward.

RITE OF PASSAGE PARENTING

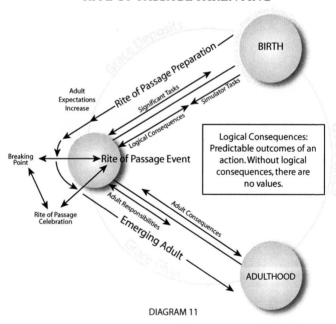

DIAGRAM 11

The cultural shift has moved so far that allowing a child to miss a meal because he forgot his lunch or refusing to replace the toy he left out in the rain will bring criticism—I guarantee it. Parents who *do* permit their kids to experience logical consequences for their actions are often labeled bad parents.

And yet, I guarantee that going against the mainstream and putting logical consequences back into your kids' lives is one of the best things you will ever do for them. The logical consequences they experience now will instill qualities in them that will help them grow into capable, responsible, self-reliant adults. In other words, logical consequences help Rite of Passage Parents equip their kids for life.

Parents today have to work hard to incorporate logical consequences into kids' lives. Years ago, young people acquired predictable outcomes much more naturally. In fact, when we settled this country as a nation of immigrants, we formed communities that shared certain values, often reflecting those of a particular culture or ethnic group. Each cultural area shared a value system and a set of beliefs, all supported by logical consequences that passed to successive generations.

I see this pattern in our family. My wife's people originally came from Norway, and they settled in Wisconsin. Actually, they pronounced it *Visconsin*. They had their own Norwegian traditions, values, and beliefs that they shared and passed down through the years.

My family, however, is Irish. I got my first name from my grandfather, Walker Winfield Scott, whose father came straight from Ireland. In fact, as I grew up, everything in my life was Irish. I just knew that the beloved Lassie that I watched every week on television was a good Irish dog, *Father Knows Best* showed us a strong Irish family, and even my hero, Superman, was (you guessed it) Irish.

In our rural Irish community in Missouri, we had a rule: any parent could spank any child. For young children, spanking is an immediate, obvious logical consequence. Since the members of our community shared the same value system and very similar beliefs, if one parent thought an action was wrong, the rest also considered it wrong. In fact, if anyone came into our community who looked or acted differently than we did, we didn't understand him. We were Irish, our families were Irish, and our values were Irish.

As we have seen, when our culture shifted after World War II and we moved from an agricultural to an industrial society, things began to change. Suddenly, people began to move to places where they could find jobs instead of staying where their cultural value systems surrounded and nurtured the growth of their children. Some of the Norwegians moved to Missouri, bringing their values and beliefs along. Some of the Irish moved to Chicago, and other cultural groups with their own values and beliefs began to split up, move around, and combine.

With all this transition, our country experienced a breakdown of the close-knit communities that had helped instill moral values and beliefs into our children through logical consequences. Since these different cultural groups had a hard time agreeing on which actions led to which consequences, we began to eliminate logical consequences from our kids' lives altogether. When this happened, the variety of values and beliefs expanded rapidly. For the first time, you could take your choice.

TAKE YOUR CHOICE

When I think about the way values and beliefs have multiplied because of the cultural shift, I think about my boyhood days on the Missouri farm. When my brothers and I got hot and thirsty from a long day of bucking bales or mending fences, we would head down to the corner filling station with its icebox full of Cokes. Actually, that icebox held bottles of Coke, Nehi Grape, and Dr. Pepper. I always looked at all three, but I always chose the Coke.

Today, if I stop in at the local gas station to pick up a Coke, I also have a choice to make. However, my choices have multiplied in the years since my days on the farm. Today, I can choose from Coke; Diet Coke; Coca-Cola C2; Coca-Cola Zero; Coca-Cola and Diet Coke flavored with Lemon, Lime, Vanilla, Raspberry, Cherry, Black Cherry Vanilla, or Splenda . . . the list goes on and on. And that doesn't even include all the other soft drinks with their multiple flavors and formulas! I look at each one and, bewildered by the choices, pull out . . . a Coke.

Because of the agricultural-industrial cultural shift, this generation has hundreds of choices to make—choices that continue to expand as more and more information reaches our kids through a wide variety of media and other sources. These choices extend far beyond soft drinks. When society removes the logical consequences from children's lives, it also removes the parameters that guide them into good decision making and wise choices.

It All Began in the Garden

Adam and Eve, on the other hand, had definite parameters. When God placed his children in the garden of Eden, he set up certain boundaries. He stated them very simply: "You eat . . . you die."

In other words, the logical consequence of eating the forbidden fruit was death. "Of the tree of the knowledge of good and evil you shall not eat, for in the day that you eat of it you shall surely die" (Gen. 2:17 NKJV). God said it, and that settled it.

The fruit looked so attractive that day. Eve had been walking in the garden for some time, and her hunger grew more urgent as she stopped to look around. When the crafty serpent tempted her by pointing out the tree laden with luscious fruit, she found it easy to listen to his deceptive words. "What could it hurt . . . just one little taste?"

Once Eve had made her fatal choice, it seemed only natural to share her find with Adam. Suddenly, the crisp garden air didn't smell quite as sweet, and the sparkling garden sky didn't look nearly as blue. Adam and Eve hid from their Creator, experiencing for the first time the emotions of guilt and shame—just a small part of what we know were logical consequences.

God knew. He knew all along, but when his children came out of hiding, he began to berate them in the way all good parents do. "I've told you! If I've told you once, I've told you a thousand times! How many times have I told you? *Don't eat the fruit of the tree of the knowledge of good and evil!*"

If you check out Genesis 3 or if you know your Bible, you'll realize that God said nothing of the kind. In fact, parents, if you have to tell your kids something over and over again, you're demonstrating to them that their behavior has no logical consequences. God did exactly the opposite. He set up a logical consequence, a predictable outcome of eating the fruit: "You eat . . . you die." Because of this logical consequence, when Adam and Eve chose to disobey him, they set themselves up to die—physically as well as spiritually.

SUSIE AND THE SCIENCE FAIR

Failing to allow children to experience logical consequences has helped make the annual school science fair what it is today: every parent's nightmare: You know the story because it's probably happened in your home . . . perhaps more than once.

It's Thursday night, and Little Susie is already in bed when a cry goes up from her bedroom, "Oooh nooo!"

Anxious parents: "What's wrong, honey?"

Susie: "I forgot."

Parents: "What did you forget?"

Susie: "I forgot that we have a science fair project due."

Parents: "When is it due?"

Susie: "Tomorrow."

Parents: "What? The science fair is tomorrow? Oooh nooo!"

Mom and dad get Little Susie out of bed and begin consulting all sorts of books and online resources, trying to figure out how to make a last-minute project that will astound the judges. Before long, dad heads off to Super Wal-Mart, armed with a yard-long shopping list and thanking God that the store never closes. There he meets thirty other parents, and guess what? Only moments ago, these parents, too, found out about the science fair.

Sometime after midnight, Little Susie gets so sleepy that mom and dad send her off to bed. With the project due in the morning, they have no choice but to stay up and finish it. In fact, as far as they are concerned, the project has become *their* significant task. Mom types away at the computer while dad runs the complicated experiment, using his digital camera to take pictures from various angles. They work together to prepare a brilliant display. Just before breakfast, they wearily awaken Susie, secure in the knowledge that they have shielded her from the shame of admitting to her teacher, "I forgot."

You see, I know about those all-nighters. I've been to those science fairs, and I've easily identified the projects that mom and dad put together. You know how I know? Kids don't weld nearly that smoothly!

When children do not face logical consequences for the choices they make, they learn that every choice (and every outcome) is negotiable. If a teacher gives Little Johnny a detention, his mother will go to the school and talk his teacher out of the discipline. If Little Susie fails a college course, her father will call the professor and get the F erased from her transcript. I tell parents this: "Where there are no logical consequences, there are no values."

✑

WHERE THERE ARE NO LOGICAL CONSEQUENCES, THERE ARE NO VALUES.

For a little over ten years, I served as youth minister at First Baptist Tulsa, an inner-city church. Because of our location, a number of interesting characters came through our doors. The church is located directly across the street from a Trailways station. Whenever a bus unloaded, some of the passengers typically came across the street to see what the church might have to offer in the way of food, money, or other help.

Our church contained the richest of the rich and the poorest of the poor, and my youth ministry reflected the same thing. One of the students in my youth group could open a locked car and start it within seconds. In fact, he was so good at this that he demonstrated his skills . . . fifty-two times. After his arrest, he was taken to juvenile court. Since he was so young, the court decided not to prosecute him or do anything else about the stolen vehicles.

The young man learned a lesson from this experience. Since he experienced no logical consequences for hot-wiring and driving fifty-two cars, he learned to continue his life of crime. Where there are no logical consequences there are no values.

Our society reflects that truth from top to bottom. During the OJ Simpson trial, I was living in Budapest, Hungary. My

Hungarian friends all told me the same thing, "You Americans can get away with anything. The more money you have, the less pain you experience." They were talking about logical consequences.

Little children have no trouble learning about logical consequences, as long as parents are willing to provide them. If you put your hand on a hot stove, it hurts. You assign a value (good or bad) to an activity (putting your hand on a hot stove). The logical consequence of putting your hand on a hot stove is that your hand gets burned. Once you know that, you keep your hands away from hot stoves.

Through my work, I have spent time in Muslim cultures. In the open-air markets in Muslim cities, you will find gold necklaces, chains, and bracelets freely displayed, yet none of them ever disappear. The parameters are established well ahead of time: if you take any of the gold jewelry—in fact, if you take *anything*—you get your hand chopped off. Everyone knows that, including potential thieves. That culture has instilled strong logical consequences that have molded the society's values, beliefs, and behaviors.

CONSTRUCTION ZONE

For a moment, I want you to imagine your child's life as a building project with you, the parent, as the contractor. Although God is the Architect and Builder, you supervise the various subcontractors who work with you. In the case of your child, you are especially concerned with the building's infrastructure: matching right values with the right beliefs to produce the right kind of life. After all, you are not concerned with building a *child*—you are shaping a capable, responsible, self-reliant *adult*.

BUILDING PROJECT

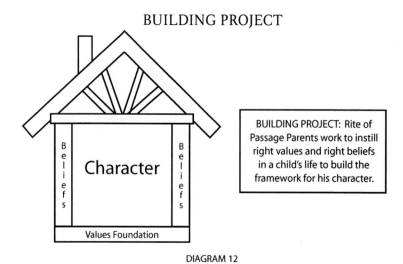

BUILDING PROJECT: Rite of Passage Parents work to instill right values and right beliefs in a child's life to build the framework for his character.

DIAGRAM 12

Let's look at the components of this building. As the contractor, you need to lay a foundation made of *right values*—those underlying principles that guide your family's life. Next, you add *right beliefs*—thoughts expressed as actions—on top of the values. Right values and right beliefs combine to build the framework for your child's *character*, the moral core that defines his identity. When the foundation and walls do not line up, cracks appear.

Today's culture brings beliefs and values into a child's life that may not match the foundation that the parents laid down at all—even if that foundation has been constructed of right values. I'll tell you more about those construction flaws in the next chapter, but if you build a foundation from right values and don't allow your kids to experience logical consequences as you go, the little flaws become big problems.

⤖ VALUES: The things that an individual deems worthy or prizes.

- ❖ BELIEFS: Thoughts expressed as actions.
- ❖ CHARACTER: Moral core that defines an individual's identity.

Mom and dad—wake up. If you don't go back and lay a values foundation in your kids' lives that is based on the will and the Word of God, then add right beliefs by using logical consequences to support them, the building you're supervising will never stand. In fact, logical consequences are an important part of the construction methods designed by the Architect and Builder. Let's get back to what he says and line up our kids' lives in accordance with his blueprints.

⟨ RITE OF PASSAGE PARENTING SUMMARY ⟩

Logical consequences, the predictable outcomes of an action, are gradually disappearing from kids' lives. All too often, our culture assumes that parents themselves or even the government should assume the logical consequences for children's actions. As a result, parents who allow their children to experience logical consequences are often branded bad parents.

Although we settled our country in communities based around similar values and beliefs, the cultural shift has removed these supportive communities and their mutually accepted logical consequences. This began when people moved toward jobs and away from extended family. Without logical consequences, kids today will have difficulty making wise choices from among the multiplicity of values and beliefs surrounding them. As a result, their character construction is faulty and their lives end up in need of constant repair.

༽

CHAPTER EIGHT

HOW IT SHOWS:
"WHAT WERE YOU THINKING?"

*Kids today often make poor choices because our culture
has failed to designate their values and beliefs as either
right or wrong.*

Once, when I had been invited to work in China for a
few weeks, I was the guest of honor at a diplomatic
banquet. I knew that my hosts considered me very important
because they seated me next to the oldest person there. She
looked as though she must be at least 180 years old! Because
the Chinese hold elderly people in high esteem, they had
deliberately placed me next to this aged woman to show their
regard for their guest from America.

The banquet arrived in thirteen separate courses—none
of them the rice that we typically associate with Chinese food.
When the first course arrived, I looked eagerly down at my
plate. *What were these strange things?* Hmmmm . . . chicken
claws! That's why they looked familiar. Back on the farm in
Missouri, I'd seen what now appeared on my plate running
around the barnyard or scratching eagerly in the dirt.

Like any good student of culture, I watched those around

me to get my cues about proper behavior. I saw the old lady pick up a chicken claw and begin sucking on the fat that surrounded each segment. She obviously enjoyed it; in fact, she began loudly smacking her lips.

That's strange, I thought. *If I had tried that back at home, my mom would have . . .* However, I knew that to avoid offending anyone, I not only needed to *observe* but to *imitate* those around me. By this time, the old lady was not the only one smacking her lips. I picked up a chicken claw and began sucking and smacking with the rest. Mom must have taught me well because I had a difficult time practicing what, according to Missouri standards, was rude behavior.

Before I had quite finished the chicken claw delicacy, the waiters carried in the next course: raw squid. I continued watching my fellow guests so as to avoid embarrassing myself. The lip smacking continued and was soon followed by something much noisier. My elderly friend opened her mouth and released a belch that rocked the room. The only reason, I was sure, that others did not turn and stare was because they were too busy belching. My youth ministry background had prepared me well. I felt as though I was back at a junior high lock-in.

Again, Mom didn't raise me to smack my lips or belch after eating. She did raise me to do something else, however, and I was ready to practice it. Like every good mother back in the 1950s, Mom raised me to *clean my plate.* In fact, because of my mother, I felt a strange connection to the Chinese people. For years, she had urged me to clean my plate because "children are starving in China." I just knew that the people there would rise up and call me blessed. After all, through the years, I had cleaned thousands of plates on their behalf. Actually, I had always wondered what possible difference could my clean plate in Missouri make all the way in China? Mom never told me, but she did keep making me clean my plate.

As I choked down the squid, I noticed that everyone around me had already started on the next course. For some reason, however, the waiter took my empty plate and brought me back more squid. I choked it down, too, but before I could quite finish, he whisked my plate away. Another waiter delivered the third course, so I could finally begin to catch up with my fellow diners.

It didn't take me long to figure it out—especially since another guest took pity on me and explained. Mom raised me to believe that plate cleaning was a sign of courtesy. In China, however, it meant just the opposite. A clean plate meant you were rude. You were effectively telling your host that he needed to provide you with even more food—that the meal was somehow unsatisfactory or insufficient. I watched, and after every course, the other guests left at least a little food on their plates. I became convinced that if someone from China had only three grains of rice on his plate, he would eat two and leave one.

Value Judgment

This experience in courtesy helped me to distinguish between *values* and *beliefs*. Let's review our definitions: a *value* is something you deem worthy or prize. A *belief*, on the other hand, refers to something you think and then carry out. It's a thought wedded to an action.

When I went to China, I held several values about meals. The first was having good food (one of my longest-held values). I also held the value of complimenting the cook who prepared good food. Finally, I valued honoring the host through the use of polite actions that we call *manners*.

My wonderful Chinese hosts shared my values: good food, honor to the one who prepared it, and good manners. Although they held the same right values that I did, they had very different beliefs. My beliefs told me that smacking lips, belching loudly, and leaving food on my plate were rude. I had to look beyond what *seemed* like wrong beliefs (because they were actually just different than my own) to see a foundation of right values. Otherwise, I might have looked at my dear Chinese friends and said, "What were you *thinking?*"

As I studied youth culture and prayed about my boys, I knew what I wanted. I wanted to raise them according to the right values and right beliefs that our family held. In fact, if I hadn't worked hard to give them logical consequences for their behavior, they would still be burping and smacking their lips after every meal. Cathy and I intentionally put logical consequences into our sons' lives so they would learn to act appropriately in our culture—and Chinese parents do the same thing. I can picture it now: "Wah Sing, that belch was too quiet! And you only licked your fingers twice. Now show us some good manners, or we'll have to take away your chicken claws."

Where there are no logical consequences, there are no values. In fact, logical consequences will clearly designate the difference between right and wrong, preparing your children to make wise choices. The proper use of logical consequences will help ensure that your children have right beliefs and right values, equipping them for life.

RIGHT VALUES, WRONG BELIEFS

Before the cultural shift that caused the dissolution of many ethnic communities, parents and children shared the same values and beliefs, and the community around them supported both. Today, even when family members share similar values, the modern world bombards children with all sorts of incompatible beliefs. The fact that many kids choose to adopt these strange beliefs as their own is the cause of much family conflict.

Mom and dad, it's not your fault. The cultural shift has brought such a wide range of beliefs into the average home that now we see even kids raised in church suddenly showing up in Gothic clothes, watching inappropriate shows, and running around with friends who do not share their faith-based beliefs. Even if we have laid a foundation of right values into our kids' lives, the wrong beliefs promoted by our culture encourage them to act in ways we could never have anticipated.

Even with a foundation of right values, parents and children alike can hold multiple wrong beliefs that guide their conduct. This mismatch causes both inner and outer conflict, forcing the individual to justify wrong actions. To return to our building analogy, they resort to *props*—statements of false thinking or faulty logic that enable someone to rationalize his or her choices.

⤙ PROPS: Statements of false thinking or faulty logic used to justify wrong beliefs or wrong values.

For example: one student values sexuality (a right value). Therefore, she believes in waiting until marriage to have sex (a right belief). Another student also values sexuality—and therefore, she believes she should only have sex with someone who "loves" her (right value, wrong belief). As long as she is in love, she can justify having sex.

One student values good grades (right value), so he believes he must work hard in school (right belief). Another student also values good grades, so he believes he must cheat to ensure a high GPA (right value, wrong belief). He justifies his actions because he understands good grades to be the surest way to a secure future.

However, the future is not bright . . . in either case. Scripture says, "For as [a man] thinks in his heart, so is he" (Prov. 23:7 NKJV). Because these students have not learned to distinguish between right and wrong beliefs through properly experiencing logical consequences, the effects will be even more devastating when their rationalizing props are ultimately pulled away. When this occurs, their building will collapse.

As the boys grew, Cathy and I worked to raise our children according to the will of God, as revealed in his Word. This is the only reliable source of universally right values and right beliefs. We worked hard to instill these right beliefs and values into their lives, and we fought hard against those that were contrary to its wisdom.

Under Construction

Think back to our building project analogy once more. Remember that God has designated you, the parent, as the contractor of your child's character; it is your responsibility to be on the job every day, watching to make sure the subcontractors do their work well.

Years ago, contractors had it easy. There were fewer subcontractors, and they all shared the same values and beliefs: the teachers, the next-door neighbors, even the clerks at the corner grocery store—all the people with whom kids came in contact. But when values-based communities began to disintegrate as people moved to find work, the force of shared values and logical consequences grew weaker and weaker. The media and technology explosions, on the other hand, added an entirely new set of subcontractors with near constant input into our kids' lives. Now, the Internet, television, movies, CDs, DVDs, MP3s, and more pull in all sorts of varying beliefs. No wonder our kids have trouble choosing between right and wrong.

Every construction job needs a good contractor, and our kids' characters are no exception. Yet somehow, in contemporary culture, the parents' role is gradually diminishing. We don't want to hurt our kids' feelings, so we allow them to watch a popular television show that has sexual overtones. We don't want to damage their self-esteem, so we buy them each a toy every time we visit the store. We fear being accused of abuse, so we hesitate to discipline them. We don't even like to say no. After all, we're supposed to keep them happy, aren't we?

Columnist Betsy Hart calls the psychologists and physicians who advocate this type of child-centered living the "expert" parenting culture. Her book *It Takes a Parent: How the Culture of Pushover Parenting is Hurting Our Kids—and What to Do About It* encourages parents to go against the flow. She raises serious concerns about a culture that encourages parents to idolize their kids.

One of the more compelling illustrations in Hart's book comes straight from the front page of the *Wall Street Journal*, where, in an article entitled, "Need Help with a Cranky Kid? Frazzled Parents Call a Coach," writer Barbara Carton tells the story of three-year-old Ellen Griswold, who began throwing temper tantrums and answering her mother rudely. Her frazzled mother quickly called for reinforcements in the form of a local parenting coach.

After months of working with a coach in person, by phone and online, Ms. Griswold is a satisfied customer. To curb Ellen's frequent tantrums when leaving the house, the coach suggested offering dress-up items, such as a tiara, which the preschooler would get to wear after they successfully departed the house. "It eliminated the meltdowns," says Ms. Griswold, who spent about $150 on the coach. "It was worth every penny."[1]

Because of the pressures of the surrounding culture, many parents today have decided that the position of contractor is too much to handle. They are parenting by default, and the subcontractors can construct anything they want in these young lives. No one stands at the door to inspect the quality of their materials (values) or their workmanship (beliefs). No one makes sure that the walls stand straight and true. The plumb line is broken—do you see it swinging wildly back and forth?

Since the contractors didn't really do their job, they can never leave the building. They've got to hang around, fixing one room or another, constantly propping up or repairing areas that weren't properly built in the first place. They now become not just helicopter parents but *handymen on demand*, providing quick fixes for the many problems that come up as their kids move into adulthood.

Kids who grow up without logical consequences typically fail to reach responsible adulthood because of the incompatible values and beliefs used in their construction. No wonder McDonald's Kids have such a hard time standing alone or finding and fulfilling the purposes the Architect and Builder has designed. Their foundation mixes right and wrong values, they hold to multiple beliefs supported by props of false thinking, and they don't know how to make wise choices. You might say that their lives won't pass inspection.

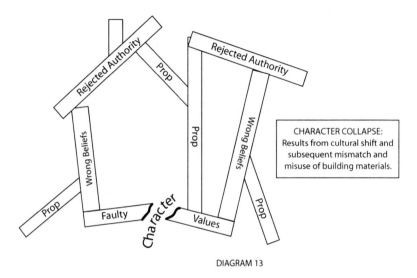

DIAGRAM 13

VALUABLE AND NONVALUABLE

As Rite of Passage Parents raise their kids, they teach them to make wise choices that will build healthy lives. These lives are capable, responsible, self-reliant, and include logical consequences that teach them how to evaluate choices and make wise decisions. Teaching your kids to know the difference between *valuable* and *nonvaluable* through the use of logical consequences is one of the best investments that you as a parent will ever make.

For instance, God's promise to children instructs them to "obey your parents in the Lord, for this is right. 'Honor your father and mother,' which is the first commandment with promise: 'that it may be well with you and you may live long on the earth'" (Eph. 6:1–3 NKJV). Children need to understand that obeying parents is valuable. Parents provide protection and direction. Disobeying parents, however, is nonvaluable. God demonstrated this in the logical consequences he established: obey your parents—it will be well with you, and you will live long. Disobey your parents, and your life will be neither as good nor as long. Understanding the logical consequences helps a child make wise choices.

I've spent some time talking with the prostitutes and drug addicts in the Red Light District of Amsterdam, and each has a story to tell about bad choices. Not one of them started out thinking, *I want to be a prostitute when I grow up. No, what I'd really love is to be a drug addict!* Instead, they all had dreams of something good and great.

None of these young men and women understood that they needed to evaluate every choice along the way, deciding whether it was good or bad, valuable or von-valuable. Some of them have told me about a bad choice they made at age twelve or thirteen that led to them, at twenty-two, selling their body on the street. They explained how the choice to take that first hit of heroin got them addicted, and how the drug became their master, driving them to use, deal, steal . . . anything to fulfill their insatiable craving for more and more.

> ↬ Valuable: Deemed worthy, prized.
> ↬ Nonvaluable: Deemed unworthy or unimportant.

The 1960s philosophy said, "Try it—you'll like it!" Today, kids think they have the option to try anything they want. However, the Enemy knows that if they try it, they'll get hooked. And since our culture blocks or delays logical consequences, kids get too far down the wrong road before experiencing the effects of their choices. At that point, lives may already be broken.

The Enemy works hard to win control over our kids' lives. Let's examine four areas where he is busily at work.

Language

Language is usually the first area where kids make choices between valuable and nonvaluable. What two-year-old doesn't quickly catch on to the power of *no* and *mine*?

When our sons were young, we decided to send them to a school on the other side of town. We had to drive them there and back, but we believed that attending this school would serve as an important cross-cultural experience. The families whose children attended that school had lives very different than ours. Although we knew we might see some fallout, nothing could have prepared us for what happened.

Why is it that kids always choose the worst moments to commit their best—and most offensive—sins? On this occasion, my Grandma Moore had come to visit. I had always thought of her as an honorary fourth member of the Trinity—Father, Son, Holy Spirit, and Grandma Moore. She was a Bible-thumping, godly grandmother, and Cathy and I were thrilled to have her in our home. On this occasion, Jeremiah came in from kindergarten with his little book bag, excited to show his great-grandmother what he had learned that day. As he trotted over to her chair, he said excitedly, "Grandma, how the _____are you doing?"

Grandma Moore immediately began praying aloud over this wayward child. I watched, amazed and embarrassed, as she looked him up and down, backward and forward, casting out demons as she went. What on earth had happened to our sweet, obedient little boy?

Jeremiah was certainly not alone in his early acquisition of foul language. Our culture seems to provide it everywhere kids turn. A 2004 Parents Television Council's report about the state of the television industry found "an increase in foul language in 2002 on virtually every network and in virtually every time slot—including the so-called 'Family Hour' of 8:00–9:00 p.m. ET/PT."[2] The same report also stated, "The teen-targeted WB network had a 188 percent increase in foul language during the family hour between 1998 and 2002. Such language increased by 308.5 percent during the second hour of prime time."[3]

It should come as no surprise that the language problem extends to MTV as well.

> Young children watching MTV are subjected to roughly 8.9 unbleeped profanities per hour, and an additional 18.3 bleeped profanities per hour. By contrast, the ten o'clock hour on the broadcast networks averaged only 6.5 uses of foul language per hour, according to the PTC's latest research. . . . Music videos contained more foul language and violence than MTV's series or specials. In the 109 hours of music video programming contained within the study period, analysts recorded 3,483 uses of foul language (32 instances per hour).[4]

What had happened to Jeremiah is what has happened to our culture. After the bright red color left my face and my blood pressure began returning to normal, I reassured Grandma that Jeremiah had *not* learned this word in our home. Finally, I began to think about how I should respond. This was the beginning of a process of teaching our sons the difference between valuable and nonvaluable language (see chapter 9).

Possessions

I hear it all the time: "Kids just don't understand the value of a dollar any more." I believe it goes way beyond the dollar. Kids have never learned the difference between things that are valuable and things that are nonvaluable. They live in a materialistic culture that throws everything away. When everything is bigger and better, it's hard to know what's valuable.

John-Boy had no trouble knowing what was valuable in his life. His family worked hard for what they had. If the crops didn't do well that year, they had less food on their table. That made every row of corn and every hill of potatoes valuable. If the cow dried up, John-Boy and his siblings had no milk to drink. That cow was valuable. If the old truck broke down, Pa had to spend time fixing it and John-Boy had to miss school to take on the extra chores. John-Boy knew the truck was valuable too.

Today, our kids begin life with piles of possessions. They receive more and more and more at birthdays, at Christmas time, and often for no special reason. They have their own bedrooms, often fully stocked with their own telephones, televisions, and computers. Their parents drive them to music lessons or soccer or cheerleading in shiny new cars while talking on the latest cell phones—and before long, the kids have the latest cell phones and even shiny new cars of their own. If the kids lose the cell phones or wreck the cars, most parents quickly replace them. Is it any wonder our kids don't know what's valuable? Everything is disposable and easily replaceable. Nothing has real value anymore. It's nonvaluable.

One parenting Web site has even coined a term for this aspect of youth culture:

Psychiatrists say we're raising a generation that is spoiled, materialistic, and bored. It often starts with well-meaning parents who want to give their kids every advantage . . . and ends with kids who believe that what they have is more important than who they are.

There's even a name for it: *Affluenza*. There is also a cure. Again, it starts with parents.

"What parents have to do first is be aware that this is as bad for their children as feeding them candy every day," says Dr. Peter Whybrow, psychiatrist and neuroscientist.[5]

Writing against what she calls the modern "parenting culture" that caters to its children regardless of cost, columnist and author Betsy Hart agrees:

Even middle-class youngsters . . . are getting too darn much stuff. Toys, electronic gadgets, cell phones—it's over the top. Many parents who can afford to give their kids these things are, it seems, beginning to see that such largesse creates selfishness, a sense of life being handed to a child on a silver platter, a presumption that a child is owed such things. Lately, parenting books and magazines are full of admonitions against giving too many material goods to children of all ages. We're beginning to hear, even from the parenting culture, that denying a child material goods he doesn't need can have incredibly positive therapeutic benefits.[6]

When our boys were young, we had the same problem many families have. Their possessions, particularly their clothes, ended up scattered all over the floor in their bedrooms or left on the couch in the den. This problem helped us devise a way to teach them the difference between valuable and nonvaluable possessions. It all began with teaching them to clean up their rooms.

If you could learn how to get your kids to clean up their bedrooms once and for all, wouldn't it be worth the price of this book and more? Most parents and students tell me that major family conflicts involve this very issue. When kids leave their belongings all over the place, they show that they don't consider them valuable. Since they don't consider anything in their room worth taking care of, they don't take care of it. In the next chapter, I'll share what we did to erase this problem and its effects from our family life and how you can do the same thing.

Finances

Again, it's a familiar story. Mom and dad get a phone call from their college-age son or daughter. Emergency, 911! The checking account is overdrawn! The science fair scene repeats: same characters, different focus. Now these helicopter parents rush to the bank, transfer money, and do whatever they can to rescue their child from the logical consequences of financial irresponsibility.

Consider the following example, taken from the files of investment and estate planning experts, about a couple they advised who were still supporting a single daughter in her early thirties:

> The family developed a budget plan that phased out parental financial support over a four-year period . . . When the plan was announced . . . it was greeted with tears and hostility . . . [but] by the end of the fourth year, [their daughter] was completely self-supporting.[7]

Would you consider this a success story? I think it's a sad but perfect example of an all-too-common phenomenon, the *spirit of entitlement.* Since we have not given our kids logical consequences, they think that someone else should come and bail them out of any financial (or other) problems. My grandparents thought they should pay their own way—and took pride in doing so. Today's McDonald's Kids and B2Bs have no problem asking, even demanding, help from mommy and daddy.

> ❧ SPIRIT OF ENTITLEMENT: An individual's belief that he is owed money, time, possessions, etc. as a function of mere existence: "I am; therefore you owe me."

Here's what the estate planning experts say:

Many children growing up in affluent homes have the notion that money grows on trees; that they have so much that they will never run out, and that, if they do, they can magically grow some more. As a result, they are incapable of exercising restraint when they receive money.[8]

One high school guidance counselor with twenty-six years of experience has definite thoughts about this topic:

Parents have abdicated their parental responsibilities and instead become their child's friend and financial backer. It is rare to have a parent with high expectations, a set of structured rules, and a strong moral foundation to guide their child.

My observation tells me that this coming generation is the most spoiled and least thankful of any generation thus far. They expect everyone to give them everything. We are destroying our future generations by taking away from them the value of having to earn what they value.[9]

Parents, if you don't fix this, your children will always struggle with making ends meet. Because of the spirit of entitlement, they won't understand that it doesn't make sense to buy a wide-screen TV on an eighteen-inch-screen budget. In chapter 9, I'll teach you how to "fix it, brother!" for this important area too.

SEXUALITY

The problem with sexuality in the days since the cultural shift can be summed up very simply: *loss of innocence*. At birth, God gives every person one gift to share with another person: the gift of innocence. Innocence is what Satan stole from Adam and Eve back in the garden of Eden, and it is what he is trying to take away from your kids too.

> ↝ LOSS OF INNOCENCE: Corruption of one or more aspects of purity in body, mind, soul, or spirit.
> ↝ INNOCENCE: Purity in body, mind, soul, and spirit.

By manipulating the media input that enters our children's lives every day, the Enemy is causing a loss of innocence through the explosion of sexual content in television, movies, and music. Consequently, children are acquiring what we used to consider adult knowledge at very young ages. The natural curiosity that young children have about sexuality has become an unnatural interest due to the proliferation of such things as Internet pornography. These tools of Satan cause a loss of innocence—a loss that can never completely be regained.

A particular danger of this loss lies in the tendency to equate sexuality with guilt. As Christian culture specialist George Barna points out, "Almost one out of every ten teenagers had sexual intercourse prior to his or her thirteenth birthday, and that number is steadily rising."[10] Small wonder that he also notes, "The gifts of childhood that have become or are rapidly becoming extinct include innocence, civility, patience, joy and trust."[11]

When the world confronts our kids with sexual images or information, they experience guilt and shame. As the process continues, they become emotionally numb—but guilt constantly lurks below the surface. On their wedding day, their sexuality has become so saturated with guilt that building a healthy relationship with their mate may take years. By robbing our children of their innocence, the Enemy has also stolen something equally precious—something that God intended to enhance the intimacy of the couple with one another and with himself.

Yes, we have traded beauty for ashes and health for hookups.

> ⚬ Friends with Benefits: Bond characterized by the provision of sexual favors for one another without the complications of a romantic relationship.
> ⚬ Hookups: An even more impersonal bond than friends with benefits, characterized by the provision of sexual favors with little or no emotional involvement.

Friends with benefits and *hookups* are two modern terms that illustrate the loss of innocence so prevalent in our world since the cultural shift. Fourteen-year-old Caity and her best friend Kate, also fourteen, live it. Their words hint at pain and guilt as Caity tells the interviewer that she is a virgin but sometimes "hooks up."

> Caity doesn't make clear what she means by "hooking up." The term itself is vague—covering everything from kissing to intercourse—though it is sometimes a euphemism for oral sex . . . [Kate has] had a boyfriend for a couple of months, but they haven't even kissed yet.
>
> [Since] . . . oral sex is common by eighth or ninth grade, and . . . hookups may skip kissing altogether, Kate's predicament strikes her friends, and even herself, as bizarre. "It's retarded," she says, burying her head in Caity's shoulder. "Even my mom thinks it's weird."[12]

Our kids will pay the price for their loss of innocence. Since the pendulum of physical maturity and the pendulum of adult responsibility are swinging farther and farther apart, they will have to wait longer and longer from the time of puberty until the time when they have the opportunity to marry and begin the sexual relationship God intends for them. For example, if they start having sexual experiences at age thirteen, but don't marry until age twenty-six, they will bring thirteen years of guilt and shame into their marriage. That's a terrible price to pay for the loss of innocence.

In the next chapter, we will look at ways you can contract with your children so they can get a grip on each of these four critical areas: language, possessions, finances, and sexuality, restoring the value that God intends for each one. If you can lay a firm foundation of right values and right beliefs in all four areas, you will have a much better chance of raising an adult whose life is built to stand firm amid cultural storms.

⌐[RITE OF PASSAGE PARENTING SUMMARY]⌐

Cultural confusion is at such an all-time high that even kids whose parents work to raise them right end up making unwise choices. Media and technology have added multiple sources of values (things that an individual deems worthy) and beliefs (thoughts expressed as actions) to kids' lives. Parents' failure to give their kids logical consequences often leads them to make poor choices based on wrong values and/or wrong beliefs. In addition, many young adults operate with a spirit of entitlement, believing parents owe them time, money, or possessions.

Allowing kids to properly experience logical consequences helps them to distinguish between valuable and nonvaluable in at least four key areas: language, possessions, finances, and sexuality. Wise choices in the area of sexuality help prevent the loss of innocence. Without the proper use of logical consequences to determine values, parents may be tempted to chastise their kids with the phrase "What were you *thinking*?"

⤳

CHAPTER NINE

ESSENTIAL EXPERIENCE #3: BUILD THEIR DISCERNMENT THROUGH LOGICAL CONSEQUENCES

We can teach our kids to make wise choices by properly using logical consequences to build right values and right beliefs into their lives.

One day, when he was in seventh grade, Jeremiah came home from school with a sad story. "Dad," he said, "I got a problem."

"What's that, Jeremiah?" I said with genuine fatherly concern.

"My homeroom teacher gave me a detention."

Now, I never got upset when the boys got a detention. As far as I was concerned, a detention represented logical consequences for something they had done, so it always made sense.

"What did you do that gave you a detention, son?"

"Well, I was sharpening a pencil at school. I had just finished and was flipping it in my hand. It just accidentally flew up and stuck in the ceiling!"

He went on to explain that as the pencil hung there in the ceiling tile, quivering, the teacher walked in and saw it.

"So now I have a detention after school tomorrow. You need to come and pick me up."

As usual, I had my answer ready. "Jeremiah, have I not already taken care of my responsibility as a dad? Our contract says that all I have to do is get you to school and back again." Because we lived outside the district where our boys attended school, we paid fifteen dollars a month for their bus ride. "I've already paid for your ride home tomorrow."

Jeremiah had his answer ready, too, only it sounded more like a question.

"Dad—what am I going to do?"

"Well, you could try renegotiating with the teacher. Maybe she could consider an alternate form of discipline. Maybe you could find that kind janitor—you know, the one who befriends the school kids in all the movies? Maybe he would bring you home."

Jeremiah didn't appear overly impressed with any of my suggestions.

"Let's see. Maybe you could walk home. It's only three miles, and you'd have to cross a major freeway. Or . . . you could call a taxicab. Here, I'll look up the number for you." I flipped through the Yellow Pages, wrote the number down, and handed the memo to my son, confident that he would appreciate my helpful spirit.

When Jeremiah left for school the next morning, Cathy and I had no idea how he would get home. I pictured my wife jumping into her Buick, driving to the school, and following three feet behind him all the way home. I decided to come home early from work that day . . . just to make sure Jeremiah could get the full benefit of the logical consequences before him.

Three o'clock—Jeremiah's normal time to return from school—came and went, and Cathy (just like Mary when Jesus stayed behind in Jerusalem) began to worry. And then 3:30,

4:00, 4:15, 4:30 . . . finally, at 4:45, a yellow-and-black taxi pulled into the driveway.

Cathy and I peeked out from behind the curtain and watched as Jeremiah climbed out of the taxi, pulled out his little brown cowboy wallet, unzipped it, and paid the driver. I ran back to my chair and picked up the newspaper, trying to appear nonchalant. Within another moment, our son was inside the house.

"How was school today, Jeremiah?" I asked cheerfully.

He glared at me. "Five dollars and ten cents!"

About six months later, Caleb came home from school and said some words that sounded familiar: "Dad, I have a detention tomorrow."

Even if I hadn't already known better than to ask about the reason for *this* detention, I didn't have the opportunity to raise the issue. Caleb was prepared, having witnessed the logical consequences his older brother had experienced. "Dad, can I hire you to come pick me up after school?"

"Well, I don't know. How much do you think you need to pay me?"

"Five dollars and ten cents." He went to his bedroom, retrieved his wallet, and paid me the money.

The next afternoon, I drove to the school and picked him up. Leave it to Caleb. He not only understood logical consequences, but he used them to negotiate.

Pay Now, or Pay Later

Jeremiah and Caleb had both experienced logical consequences. I had already paid the bill for their transportation to and from school, so when they did something that prevented them from taking the bus home, they had to experience the logical consequences, each in his own unique style.

Where there are no logical consequences, there are no values. I much prefer my sons to experience the logical consequences of a detention and the cost of a ride home from school than a failed business or a broken marriage. When parents follow the cultural norm of shielding their kids from logical consequences, they are inadvertently setting them up to experience more severe ones later in life.

Parents, you cannot raise children without paying a price. Either you pay the price of laying down solid foundations and putting good building materials into their lives early on through logical consequences, or you spend the rest of your days trying to fix their lives. Would you prefer to be a contractor or a handyman on demand?

When I teach conferences, parents come up to ask, "Where were you when I was raising my kids? I've spent my whole life trying to fix not only my children but my grandchildren as well. Our culture was shifting, and we didn't know it."

Our microwave society prefers to get things done quickly, not thoroughly. We want to substitute expediency for sound child-rearing principles. Even if your children are older, it's not too late to put logical consequences back into their lives and begin to rebuild. You can pay now or pay later . . . but you don't want to spend your whole life fixing it, brother!

CONTRACTING LOGICAL CONSEQUENCES

In order to communicate logical consequences properly to your children, you need to develop written contracts to help them understand the values you want to teach. The Bible is God's contract with us; in fact, the word *testament* means contract. We have an old contract (Old Testament) and a new contract (New Testament). God uses his contracts to communicate his values.

In the Bible, God explains things very clearly: *if* you don't do this, *this* is what will happen. From the very beginning, God always communicated clearly. Remember? "[If you eat] of the tree . . . you shall surely die" (Gen. 2:17 NKJV). They ate—and they died, first spiritually, then physically. When we contract with our children, we are giving them a written record of our values.

In each *logical consequences contract,* you will want to identify a right value you want to teach or right beliefs you wish to instill. Then you will list some things for your children to do. Of course, you'll include the logical consequences for not fulfilling the contract. As your children get older, you can negotiate those consequences, but when they are young, lay them out clearly without their input.

I recommend that you only work on *one* logical consequences contract at a time. Write it out, sign it, and have your child sign it. Then post it on that most sacred family message center: the refrigerator door.

Logical consequences contracts help parents and children because they take the emotion out of values instruction. Most of the time, we make such decisions on the spur of the moment, often when we're emotionally distraught: "Clean up your room! Now!"

I tell people that I always felt better when I spanked my children—but that wasn't really the point. You see, I'm not sure that I taught them each time a spanking occurred. By using a contract, you predetermine the logical consequences. No matter what the child chooses to do in relation to the value, there is no discussion: you've already signed the contract, so you can now point to it and say, "You did this—so this is what happens."

Let's examine some logical consequences that go along

with the four areas of values discussed in the last chapter: language, possessions, finances, and sexuality.

> ⟿ Logical Consequences Contract: A written document that matches an action(s) to right values and/or right beliefs and specifies its predictable outcomes.

Language Contract:
Good Word/Bad Word Project

Do you remember Jeremiah standing in front of Great-Grandma Moore, trying out the new word he had learned in kindergarten that day? That word became the starting point of what we called the *Good Word/Bad Word Project* and of the contract system that has served us through the years.

Before we had our contract in place, if one of the boys had said a *bad* word, I would have spanked him, washed his mouth out with soap, and grounded him. *That'll teach him*, I might have thought.

It would have taught him, all right. It would have taught him not to get caught saying the word in front of mom or dad. Instead, Jeremiah and I got together and created the Good Word/Bad Word Project.

I told Jeremiah that when God created the world, he said that everything was good. Satan takes what is good and tries to make it bad. The Enemy has done the same thing with words. Every bad word came from something good. The contract we made with Jeremiah was that he could not use any of the new words he learned at school until he came home and we discussed them together in our evening family time. We made a chart on a piece of poster board—just two columns labeled *Good Words* and *Bad Words* with a line down the middle.

When Jeremiah told us a bad word he had learned, we talked together about what it meant. I let Jeremiah, and later Caleb, decide whether the word belonged on the *good* or *bad* side of the chart, depending on its meaning and use. Although I didn't know it at the time, these discussions paved the way for the talks we needed to have later about physical development and sexual purity. I didn't have to fear bringing up these words or topics with my boys—we had begun discussing them in kindergarten.

The Good Word/Bad Word Project had a powerful impact on my sons' lives. I had no idea when I started it, however, that Jeremiah would apply transference of learning once again. He took what he had learned about language and extended it across many other areas of his life. He began assigning values—either good or bad—to every activity and experience he encountered as he made his way through elementary school. He understood what many adults do not: words and actions have value and can be identified as good or bad, valuable or nonvaluable.

POSSESSIONS CONTRACT: CLEAN YOUR ROOM!

How many times have you told your child, "Clean your room!" and returned to find it just barely improved? I imagine you've also confronted your child with an insightful parental statement like "I told you to clean your room!" She responds glumly, "I did."

When you tell a child to clean her room, you tell her from the perspective of your thirty-five or forty-four or however many years of life experience in room cleaning. However, your child hears your instructions from the perspective of her few years of life experience. Because she has cleared a path from the door to the bed or closet, she honestly believes that the room is clean. The fact that you don't agree, according to educator Stephen Glenn, is attributable to an *adultism*, something that "occurs any time an adult forgets what it is like to be a child and then expects, demands, and requires of the child, who has never been an adult, to think, act, understand, see, and do things as an adult."[1]

> ☙ ADULTISM: Something that "occurs any time an adult forgets what it is like to be a child and then expects, demands, and requires of the child, who has never been an adult, to think, act, understand, see, and do things as an adult."

Contracting logical consequences forces you to take time to clarify the objectives you have for your child, and help gradually to increase her skill level. As you build age-appropriate skills into her life, she will be able to match the goals you have set. You can use the logical consequences contract to list exactly which tasks you want performed (all toys picked up and put in their appropriate places, clothes folded and put away, room dusted, trash emptied, etc.) and how often you want each one completed (daily, twice a day, weekly, etc.).

I can hear you already: "I understand the contract, Walker. But how do I make my child clean up her room?" This is where things get interesting.

Remember that when a child leaves her belongings lying around, she is deeming them nonvaluable (i.e., not worth removing from the floor). We explained this to our boys, and told them that Tulsa had a very special store that would take these nonvaluable items and make them valuable again.

"Really, Dad? What kind of a store is it?" Caleb asked. Jeremiah, wise to the ways of his dad, waited silently.

"It's called Goodwill. The people there will determine exactly how valuable each of your nonvaluable items is, put a price tag on it, and sell it to someone who thinks it is valuable."

We didn't do it that first day, and we didn't do it every time. However, not long after we made our first logical consequences contract for possessions, Cathy and I drove to Goodwill with two unhappy little boys in the back of the car.

"Dad! You're not really going to give them our Nintendo, are you?"

"Dad! And what about my MU sweatshirt? Uncle Gary bought that for me!"

"Boys, it was in the contract—remember? You keep your clothes and toys put away properly, and I won't need to take anything to Goodwill. If you don't . . . well, you'd better start saving your money to buy back your stuff."

Caleb and Jeremiah learned a lot through the clean room contract. Although they eventually found garage-sale substitutes for some of the items we had taken to Goodwill, they were never able to completely replace what they had lost. This logical consequences contract helped them to understand the difference between valuable and nonvaluable possessions. They also began to keep their rooms clean . . . at least 51 percent of the time.

About once a year, contracts like the possessions contract need revision as your child grows and matures. You need to take the time to clarify the changing objectives you have and match them to an age-appropriate skill level. You guessed it: fulfilling this type of contract builds simulator tasks into your kids' lives, preparing them for capable, responsible, self-reliant adulthood.

FINANCES CONTRACT: DESIGNER JEANS

One day, when they were about seven and ten years old, Caleb and Jeremiah came to me, excited about the latest fashion trend. "Dad, all the kids at school are wearing these cool designer jeans! Can we get some?"

I couldn't believe it. My boys were already concerned with looking cool. "What's so great about these designer jeans?"

"Dad, they have *holes* in them!"

Being raised in rural Missouri, this concept made no sense to me. I had always thought that the reason you bought new jeans was because your *old* ones had holes in them. Suddenly, my boys were trying to convince me to buy them new jeans with . . . holes. The cost of "cool," in this case, turned out to be fifty dollars a pair.

I decided that this was a good opportunity to teach my sons the value of finances. I spent some time doing research and sat down to work out a logical consequences contract. "Boys, I know you like the designer jeans. Mom and I talked about it, and we decided that it's our responsibility to provide you with three pairs of jeans for your school year. Now, I've found some good-quality jeans with sturdy fabric and strong stitching for nineteen dollars a pair at the department store in town.

"What I'm going to do is this: I will give you the fifty-seven dollars it will cost to buy three pairs of those everyday jeans. You can buy one pair of designer jeans for fifty dollars and wear that pair to school every day this year, or you can buy three pairs of the other jeans. That way, you can rotate them and make them last. In fact, I'll make you a deal. I can even put holes in the plain jeans for you—if you want, you can call them *Walker's*." I smiled as I presented our latest logical consequences contract to the boys.

Neither Jeremiah nor Caleb returned my smile, but they signed the contract, took the money, and went off to the store with their mother. We had used the concept of a finances contract for articles of clothing before, but this was the first time they had been so concerned with fashion. I really wondered which decision they would make.

As it turned out, both the boys chose wisely. They each came home with three pairs of the more basic jeans, and I didn't have to make holes in any of them. They understood the logical consequences: if they bought the designer jeans, they would have to wear the same pair to school day after day. Buying the less-expensive jeans gave them more clothes to last through the year. In fact, if they had found jeans that cost *less* than the amount we budgeted, they could have kept the leftover money. That way, if they found bargains, they ended up with extra money for themselves.

Since the boys kept growing and needing new clothes, as kids tend to do, our family used logical consequences contracts like this every season. Cathy and I decided when they needed a new coat or shoes, and how much to budget for each item. The boys would take the full amount and do their shopping. They could easily see the logical consequences: if they chose a designer shirt or pants that took a large chunk of their allotted money, they would have to do without some other clothing item or squeeze into something they had outgrown the previous year.

These logical consequences contracts taught our boys about the value of finances. They had the opportunity to make wise decisions about their purchases rather than impulsive ones based on the emotion of the moment. In the process, our boys were learning to determine the value of finances. Cathy and I thought that was cool.

Sexuality Contract: Up-to-Date

Syndicated columnist Betsy Hart, as I pointed out earlier, has noticed a problem with the parenting culture in our country. She touches upon the symptoms by discussing the freedom we give our children:

> Experts have encouraged parents to give their little ones freedom and choices at every conceivable opportunity, or to trick their kids into thinking they are being given a choice even when they aren't. But, of course, the children don't learn how to handle freedom; they learn little more than that they're calling the shots.
>
> Flash forward to the teen years, when many parents finally realize that not only is the world a dangerous place but that children can be a danger to themselves. Often the parents panic and want to start restricting their teenager. From clothes to friends to curfews to activities, the parents might try to [place limits on behavior]. But by then the child is used to being in charge and making his own choices—he's come to see it as his "right"—so restrictions are often a losing battle.[2]

Rite of Passage Parenting provides a way out of this dilemma. Parents and kids who have properly used logical consequences to build right values and right beliefs into their kids' lives set the stage for open discussions about some of the dangers that today's teens encounter. By the time your kids reach an age where they are ready to date, in fact, you need to have *them* write the logical consequences contract.

That's what Cathy and I did. Why did we do this? First of all, Cathy and I understood the dangers of loss of innocence.

We also knew that, for this area in particular, we could not make our sons' choices for them. They would have to make their own decisions about surrendering their sexuality to the Word and will of God. Because we had worked to build right values and right beliefs into their lives through logical consequences, we knew they had the skills to choose wisely in this important area too.

Parents, your child's sexuality is not something to ignore or outsource to the school or the church. Remember, the pendulum of physical maturity is swinging earlier and earlier while the pendulum of adult responsibility is swinging later and later. You need to find ways to help your kids deal with their adult hormones and sexual feelings. If you don't pay now, you and your kids will pay later. In the area of sexuality, the costs can be especially painful.

Because we had already discussed terms and issues with our sons through the Good Word/Bad Word Project, we did not have to have "the talk" that every parent dreads. Our boys grew up learning about their sexuality in the safe environment of our home with the people we most trusted to convey right values and right beliefs: ourselves. Teens who have wrong beliefs, even built on right values foundations, often think that any sexual activity short of intercourse constitutes right behavior. We taught our sons that sexuality covers much more than intercourse. Because males are aroused by sight, merely *looking* at a girl can be a sexual experience.

Next, our family developed a chart for sexual activity and discussed each step with our boys. Once they understood this chart, each of our sons was ready to write his own sexuality contract.

I tell students that the safest place to set a definite limit on sexual behavior is before they get to kissing. That's not what they want to hear . . . but again, God has a deep concern that we protect against a loss of innocence. In the area of sexuality, teens will either pay an extreme price for wrong behavior or earn incredible rewards for right behavior. When they move past hand holding, they experience a loss of innocence one step at a time.

ASSIGNING VALUES TO SEXUALITY

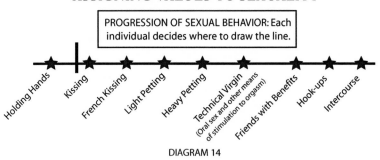

DIAGRAM 14

The sexuality contract included much more than just sexual information. We asked our sons to consider when, who, and how they would date. We taught them that dating meant beginning the process of finding the mate God intends for them. Therefore, we emphasized the value of dating only believers, and we did not allow them to date before they turned sixteen. Studies show that the earlier kids begin dating, the more likely they are to become sexually involved.[3]

When our boys were ready to begin dating, they knew whom they should date, and they knew where they wanted to draw the line on sexual behavior. In fact, Jeremiah came to me when he was fourteen years old, saying he had made a decision. "What's that, son?" I asked.

"I'm going to keep myself pure until marriage."

This was a decision that I could not make for Jeremiah, and, of course, it pleased me very much. The reason he did not date during high school (except for his senior prom) went back to this commitment made during his freshman year.

The proper use of logical consequences, based on right values and right beliefs, has helped many young people make the choices that allow them to enjoy a healthy dating life. Students who do not have a predetermined plan that allows them to set boundaries ahead of time have a difficult time setting those boundaries at all. Rite of Passage Parents know that ultimately, they cannot set the guidelines for their sons' or daughters' sexual behavior. Instead, these parents give guidance so that the students are equipped to make their own responsible choices, set their own guidelines, and enjoy wholesome, guilt-free relationships.

CALEB'S STORY

For every truth that God has shown me, he tests me. I would never have anticipated that the greatest challenge to my teaching would come through the choices of our youngest son. In his late teens and early twenties, Caleb decided to test the waters and reject his parents' values and beliefs. He went out from under our authority and began a journey completely on his own.

One morning at 3:00 a.m., I got a phone call from the Tulsa Police Department. Everyone hates those early-morning calls, not knowing who it is or what the problem might be.

I picked up the phone. "Hello."

"Mr. Moore? We have your son Caleb. He was in a high-speed chase, trying to outrun the police department. We finally caught him and pulled him over to the side of the road. We're about three blocks from your house, and we have him handcuffed.

"Mr. Moore, your son keeps telling us, 'Call my dad. He's the chaplain for the police department.'"

When this event occurred, I *was* serving as a chaplain for the Tulsa Police Department, spending many hours and long nights working with suicides and other crises. "Can you come over and talk to us?"

I slipped on my clothes, including my police jacket, and walked the few blocks to where they held Caleb: drunk, handcuffed, and lying spread out on the trunk of the police car.

One of the police officers recognized me. "Chaplain Moore, you've helped us out so much, but we need to decide what to do with your son." He repeated the story of the chase and said, "Because you're a chaplain, if you want, we can let him go . . . you can talk to him, maybe help him."

"What are you *supposed* to do?" I asked quietly.

"We're supposed to arrest him and take him to jail."

I then said some of the hardest words I've had to say in my life: "Take him to jail."

When Caleb heard me, he twisted and stood up from the back of the police car. Looking straight at me, his blue eyes blinded by rage and alcohol, he forced out four words: "I hate you, Dad."

The police hauled him off to jail, and I headed home as sad and lonely as I had ever been. My son had made a choice, and as much as it hurt me, I knew he had to experience the results of his actions. Where there are no consequences, there are no values.

At this point, I had been teaching Rite of Passage Parenting principles for twenty-five years. I knew that everything I had lived and taught was being put to the test there in that jail cell.

In case you haven't noticed, Caleb is a lot like me. No matter what happens, he always has a story. These are his words:

Late one evening, the sister of one of my closest friends called me. She was crying and begging me to come pick him up. They had argued, and he had become violent . . . There was no use in trying to resolve the conflict at that point, so I merely convinced him to come and stay at my house for the evening until things settled down. I decided to stop and get a case of beer before heading to an old school parking lot located only a few blocks from my house.

When I bought the beer, I had to use my passport as proof of my age. I had lost my license a few months before when I was convicted of driving under the influence. Even though I was still on probation, I continued to drink and mess around with drugs. Some of my friends thought I was addicted . . . In reality, I just kept using them so I could stay in denial about all the problems in my life.

I parked my car. My friend and I sat on the sidewalk, drinking and discussing what had happened. Our serious conversation turned into laughter as the night wore on. We still had a few beers left, but my pack of smokes was empty, so we decided to head back up to the gas station. It was only a few months before I would be able to drive again legally . . . but I decided to risk it. I knew what back roads to take where there was very little—if any—traffic.

I got my cigarettes and a few extra beers. Drinking tends to exaggerate my showoff tendencies, so I shifted into drive and quickly released the clutch while flooring the gas. My little Honda skidded out of the parking lot and back into our neighborhood.

What I didn't know was that a pair of police cars

was parked across the street. The officers would have not looked at us twice except for the way I darted out of the parking lot. Suspecting that I had robbed the convenience store, they threw on their lights and headed after us.

When we saw those lights, I quickly turned a corner so my friend could ditch the open container of beer he had in his lap. The red and blue lights shot through the darkness of the quiet neighborhood. When I finally stopped, the police shoved a spotlight into my rearview mirror, making it hard for me to see. I followed their directions to step out of the car and slowly made my way over to one of the officers.

He asked me if I had stolen anything, and I was able to tell him the truth—I hadn't. However, it didn't take long for him to notice that I had consumed a few drinks. After running my license through his computer, he reminded me that not only was I not allowed to drive, but I had broken the agreement I had made with the judge about not drinking alcoholic beverages.

I did my best to talk my way out of it. I explained the situation with my friend and told the officer that I was just trying to do the right thing. The police hear these stories all the time, so I completely understood their lack of sympathy. The one thing that *did* get their attention was when I told them my father was a police chaplain who lived just down the street.

They asked for the phone number, and one of the officers stepped out of hearing range to talk to my dad. It was quickly approaching three in the morning as I waited, watching for my dad's familiar figure. I was sure he would come to my rescue. In just a few minutes, he appeared. He wore his police jacket and looked tired but official.

One of the officers watched my friend and me as his partner approached my father. They began to discuss the situation, and I counted the seconds until I could go. I had no doubt that my dad could convince them to release me into his custody. I would promise never to do it again, and that would be the end of that. I would be free.

However, as I lay on the back of the police car, giving my dad my best "Please, help me" look, I saw him mouth those dreaded words, "Take him to jail."

The officers had given my dad the choice, and he had made it. His round face, stressed and exhausted, turned toward the ground as they unceremoniously shoved us into the back of the police car. The cold metal of the cuffs grew tighter until the steel dug into my skin. I paid no attention to that. Instead, I was staring straight at my dad. The man who was supposed to have rescued me, who *could* have rescued me, had just made the decision to send his youngest son to the David L. Moss Correctional Facility.

I know my eyes said it all. But just in case he missed the message, I spoke through clenched teeth, "I hate you, Dad."

My friend had enough money to post his bail that evening, but I had to wait a little longer. This being my second offense, I was in a lot more trouble than he was. Now that I look back on it, I had it easy. Going to jail isn't all that difficult. You just put on a face as if you don't care. You start up conversations with those around you about how messed up everything is. Again, that was easy.

My parents had the hard part. I can't imagine how my mother felt the first time she saw me in jail. As if giving birth were not difficult enough, she had to talk to her baby boy through thick walls of glass or on the phones as I tried to comfort her. "It's not your fault, Mom." No good mother should have to do that—and my mom is the best.

Then there was my dad—the man who made the decision that got me hauled off, hands behind my back. He understood that this would mean a lot more than just time spent in a cell. There would be attorney's fees, court dates, and community service to deal with for a long time. He knew all of that in advance, and he still made the decision he did. Why? Because he loved me, and that kind of love is never easy.

Real love doesn't always bail the other person out. Sometimes real love steps aside so that the loved one may experience the full effect of his actions. Real love not only allows a son to go to jail but also wakes up early in the morning to drive him to his community service on the days the bus doesn't run.

My dad went with me to nearly all my hearings. Except for the times he was out of town, my mom stayed home—right where she belonged. After all, no good mother belongs at a courthouse hearing. No good mother should have to watch her son fit into the crowd of people standing there, all waiting to bargain with the judge. Still, I was glad that I never went to one of my hearings alone. Either Mom or Dad was always by my side.

For a while, I hated my dad for what he did, and I expressed that too freely on occasion. However, now that I have grown in the Lord, I pray that one day I will love my own kids the way my mom and dad love me. Making the choice my dad made was hard. If I had gone home that first night, I might still be the stupid kid, making poor decisions and destroying my family and myself.[4]

There are times when allowing your child to experience logical consequences hurts more than anything you can imagine. That night under the streetlights, I caught a glimpse of how God felt when his children turned their backs and walked out of the garden of Eden, naked and ashamed. In the next section, I'll share with you the key that began to unlock the door of Caleb's heart. Then you'll know the rest of the story.

⸙ RITE OF PASSAGE PARENTING SUMMARY ⸙

Where there are no logical consequences, there are no values.

We can teach our kids to make wise choices by adding logical consequences into their lives through the development of written contracts. These spell out the logical consequences for a particular activity matched to a right value and/or right belief.

The Good Word/Bad Word Project provides a way to contract for language by assigning a value to each word.

The possessions contract helps kids determine whether their possessions are valuable or nonvaluable—and also teaches them to keep their rooms clean.

The finances contract helps kids determine the value of finances by determining exactly how to spend a budgeted amount for a particular area of need.

The sexuality contract, developed by the emerging adults themselves, allows them to make wise decisions about their own sexual behavior.

Applying logical consequences is sometimes very difficult, but it is always right.

GRACE
DEPOSITS

⤸

CHAPTER TEN

WHAT'S MISSING:
KIDS NEED GRACE DEPOSITS

The cultural shift has left our children's lives lacking in "grace deposits"—statements or actions that communicate an individual's intrinsic worth in a way that he or she finds meaningful.

L et's look in on our old friend John-Boy. Who lives in the Walton homestead? Of course, John and Olivia Walton, their active brood of children, and John's parents, Grandma and Grandpa Walton.

I like to tell parents that it takes two things to raise a child: law and grace. In fact, it takes 49 percent law and 51 percent grace to complete the job. We'll discuss those percentages later.

- ❧ LAW: Statements or actions that lessen a child's sense of self-worth and value.
- ❧ GRACE: Statements or actions that help build a child's sense of self-worth and value.

I remember an episode of *The Waltons* in which John-Boy sat on the front porch, crying and distraught. The screen door opened, its hinges creaking as Grandpa pushed through the doorway and stepped onto the porch. He sat down beside John-Boy and put his arm around his grandson. His rough words overflowed with love as he reminded John-Boy of his importance, and of how much he appreciated having him as a grandson. Before long, John-Boy's sobs had subsided, and the pair laughed together over one of Grandpa's funny stories.

Once again, the Walton family paints a perfect picture of what has shifted in our culture, leaving an enormous gap. In an agricultural society, not only Grandma and Grandpa, but aunts, uncles, and other extended family lived close by. In every generation, mom and dad have the job of being the law. We tell our kids to sit up straight, eat their food, do their homework, and go to bed on time. The *law* side of parenting is part of the way we instill right values and right beliefs into our children. Rite of Passage Parents know that's important.

Grandparents have a different function within the family. Their primary job is to tell their grandchildren of their worth and value. I was blessed to have grandparents who did this. Every time I looked into their eyes, I saw myself as a person with potential. They knew I was going to grow up to be somebody. They believed that, they told me that, and they affirmed that in my life.

In a relatively short time, our culture has shifted so that increasing numbers of families have moved away from the people who put value and worth into their children's lives, away from the people who taught mom and dad how to be mom and dad. When the Waltons' children were growing up, it was Grandma and Grandpa who taught John and Olivia, and gave them wise advice on raising children. The episodes of

The Waltons contain many scenes where the family sat around the table and talked about decisions, problems, joys, and sorrows. The intergenerational sharing that the show portrays was commonplace before the cultural shift.

Suddenly, Grandma and Grandpa have changed. They've sold the farm, bought a Winnebago, and are on their way to Las Vegas with a bumper sticker on the back of their motor home that reads, "Out spending our children's inheritance." All of a sudden, grandparents don't want to be grandparents anymore.

WHAT'S MISSING?

Stephen Glenn explains the important role that grandparents played before the agricultural-industrial cultural shift:

> If a father disciplined his son too heavily, Grandma was often there to soothe and say, "He was like that when he was a boy, too, but you had better go along and do what he says." In this way, even the strictest, most authoritarian discipline could be moderated, given positive meaning and thus made more acceptable.[1]

Since the early 1950s, families have moved away from this extended family network with its many benefits. The separation from older generations adds to the difficulty parents experience in passing right values and right beliefs to their children. Pastor and parenting expert Jay Kesler summarizes it well when he calls grandparents "carriers of culture" who serve as connecting links to help root our society in values from the past.[2]

Today's kids have a far different experience than their grandparents did as children. Instead of spending hours every day personally involved with parents, grandparents, aunts, uncles, cousins, and other nearby relatives, they have much less interaction with a much smaller number of family members. Relatives generally live far away, and most people live in nuclear families consisting only of one or two parents plus children. It becomes easy for parents to communicate quickly, correcting problems without taking time to affirm. As Glenn says:

> Interaction within nuclear families today amounts to only a few minutes a day. Of these few minutes, more than half are not true interaction. Rather, they are one-way communications delivered in a negative tone: parents' warnings or reproaches to children for misbehavior.[3]

The lack of time and lack of input from extended family have combined to create problems not just for today's kids but for their parents as well. Without the loving, mentoring support of their own parents, mom and dad often turn to all sorts of experts to provide parenting advice and more.

> The burgeoning industry of services aimed at harried parents, which began with the likes of birthday-party packages at gyms and pizza shops, has expanded to the point where you can now hire someone to assist with everything from potty-training your toddler to getting your teenage daughter to agree to a passably modest prom dress.
>
> *Childwork*, as I would call it, is one of our economy's growth industries, as affluent parents try to balance work and family, deal with ever intensifying anxieties, and give their kids a leg up in the race for success," says

Steven Mintz, a historian at the University of Houston who specializes in childhood . . . Parents like these, who come out of a workplace culture that brings in the "experts" to tackle any problem, are sometimes inclined to seek out similar expertise in their family life.[4]

John and Olivia Walton sought out their own avenues of parenting expertise—seated out on the broad front porch, gathered around the fireplace, or exchanging ideas over the dishes after a family supper. John and Olivia paid a price for this expertise, however: a price spelled t-i-m-e. They also paid the price, at least occasionally, of conflict. The advice Grandma and Grandpa gave did not always coincide with what John and Olivia thought was right for their family and their children. Sometimes that hurt.

Nonetheless, the price the Waltons paid for their extended family relationships was much less than the seventy-five dollars per hour charged by some parenting coaches. It certainly cost less than the price that might have been paid if the Walton children had grown up without Grandma and Grandpa Walton's loving influence. That kind of personal care, concern, and wisdom is priceless.

AN EXPERIMENT IN AGING

During my days as a youth minister, I realized that the cultural shift had affected our church family. Specifically, the youth group was operating independently of the senior adult ministry. The youth went on mission trips, camp experiences, and other outings. The senior adults went on tours and tours.

Frankly, the two groups seemed to prefer their separate lives. The senior adults complained about the youth group

("They're running down the halls in the church!" "They're leaving notes all over the pews!"), and the youth group complained about the senior adults ("They're so slow!" "They expect us to be quiet, but they can't hear us unless we talk LOUD!"). Most of our young people didn't understand the importance of relating to older generations, and the older people had lost the understanding that comes from regularly interacting with those who are younger.

I designed an experiment in hopes of increasing students' understanding of the aging process. One Sunday afternoon before Valentine's Day, I gathered all the students together in the fellowship hall and began the process of transforming them. I wanted them to experience, as much as possible, what being a senior adult was really like.

First, I put large kitchen trash bags on their hands. The bags extended six to eight inches beyond the students' fingertips, and I taped each one off at the wrist. Immediately, the students lost their dexterity. They couldn't pick up anything without difficulty. They couldn't turn the pages in their Bibles. One boy excused himself for a few minutes, returning with a comment about how difficult even something as simple as using the restroom had suddenly become.

In the meantime, I placed a double layer of gauze over each student's eyes. They could see . . . but not very well. The students' posture changed. They began bending their heads forward and peering out, trying their best to see what was ahead of them through the cumbersome gauze. They looked like . . . senior adults.

Next, I tied each student's ankles together with a short piece of rope. Now their steps became short and awkward. No one would complain about them running down the hallways of the church anymore. They couldn't even *think* about running.

That night, the youth choir sang. The students shuffled and stumbled up the stairs to the choir loft. They held the hymnals at odd angles, trying their best to see the words on the page and—even less successfully—the congregation. After four hours of this aging experiment, the students begged to remove the various items that had added fifty years or more to their young bodies. Now that they understood what it felt like to be a senior adult, they were ready to return to being young.

The next night, the students visited all the senior adults in the church and delivered flowers for Valentine's Day. One of our young women, Katherine, ended up at a nursing home. As she reached out to take a lady's hand, the older woman warned her, "Be careful! I have arthritis right there, and it hurts!"

"Oh, I *know* arthritis hurts!" Katherine answered with understanding. "I had it yesterday!"

The experiment in aging worked so well that we repeated it every year. Now that they knew the young people understood the challenges they faced, the senior adults began to talk to them. Once the students knew they were accepted, they began to talk to the senior adults more openly. For the first time, relationships developed between the two groups. The need for this interaction extended in both directions.

The young people began to find encouragement and acceptance from the senior adults that they often lacked in other areas of life. Suddenly, I had no trouble raising funds to take twenty students on an overseas mission trip. Although few of the senior adults could *go* themselves, they could *give*—and they did—to the young people they now considered their adopted grandchildren.

Again, the benefits extended both ways. Once, I sent the students out with a set of questions to ask their senior adult friends. The visits were supposed to take thirty minutes but lasted more like two hours. Almost every group came back laughing. One of the questions dealt with what had first attracted the senior adult to a future mate. One of the young men told us, "He said she had sexy ankles! Back then, that must've been all he could see!"

This type of caring intergenerational relationship was natural during the days of the Walton family. In fact, it is the normal life that God intended, in which the younger person respects and honors the older, and the older person respects and nurtures the younger. By segregating our society, we have missed this biblical model. By missing intergenerational relationships, McDonald's Kids are missing out.

ESSENTIAL EXPERIENCE #4: GRACE DEPOSITS

When the Columbine High School tragedy happened on April 20, 1999, people were quick to point fingers in all directions. The same thing happens with any school shooting. The media, teachers, government—it seemed everyone criticized and received blame all at once. When Colorado governor Bill Owens spoke a year after this tragedy, he asked:

> Do we truly have the courage to do what it will take to change a culture that produces such alienated and violent children? . . . Our culture is badly in need of repair and healing . . . It is clear to me that there is an answer to the cultural challenge we face. It is clear that we must once again look over the abyss, step back and strengthen our families . . . There is no institution more important to our success. Strong families are our first and most important bulwark against youth violence and other social pathologies.[5]

Yes, strengthening our families sounds great. All rite of passage parents would agree about that—but how exactly do we do it? Once again, we need to look to the old road—to the ways of the Walton family, to the days prior to the cultural shift, and especially to the ways of God. His plan is perfect, and his ways are right.

Mom and dad, you'll love this next line:

Grandparents are the downfall of America.

Of course I don't mean that grandparents cause all our problems. Instead, I say this because many of our children do not have grandparents who are willing or able to extend the caring, loving concern that their grandchildren need. As a result, many of today's kids grow up without anyone in their lives who takes on a true grandparent role. Kids who don't have grandparents in their lives miss a lot of grace.

The average child lives with lots of rules. At home, we use rules. At school, they use rules. In sports, the teams use rules. Living under lots of rules means that a child lives under law.

A person who lives completely surrounded by the constant oppression of law has a difficult time. At school, he hears the law: "Get out a pencil and paper. We're having a pop quiz. Read the next twenty-five pages before tomorrow. Do not run in the halls. Write a two-page report before the end of class today." Throughout the school day, in every class, more and more law is applied.

I like to use banking terms to describe what I call the *Checkbook Theory*. This theory states that parents can systematically and positively affirm their children through *grace deposits* into an *inner "spirit account"—a space within each individual from which he draws his self-esteem and self-worth.*

The continued application of law in the typical school scenario described above causes huge withdrawals from the child's spirit account. After the child goes home, often after experiencing more law in the after-school care program or sports team, and finally sees his parents, what's the first thing they say? "Have you done your homework? Did you get a detention? Have you cleaned up your bedroom? Did you remember to set the table?" The child hears nothing but law ... law ... law ... and suddenly, his spirit account is in the red.

Have you ever had an employer who had nothing good to say about you—for whom you could do nothing right? Do you know what happens when people work for someone like that? After a while, they have to find a release from the constant oppression of law. They begin to steal pencils, they begin to talk about the boss behind his back, and they begin to use company time to play games on the Internet, almost anything to try to find release and relief from all that law.

- ⊸ CHECKBOOK THEORY: Parents can systematically and positively affirm their children through grace deposits into an inner spirit account.
- ⊸ GRACE DEPOSITS: Statements or actions that communicate an individual's intrinsic worth in a way that he finds meaningful.
- ⊸ SPIRIT ACCOUNT: A space within each individual from which he draws self-esteem and self-worth.
- ⊸ GRACE DEFICIT: A state in which an individual's spirit account has had more withdrawals than grace deposits so that he sees himself as worthless and insignificant.

When I look at school shootings, I see individuals who lived under constant law. They had generally been in trouble before, so more law was applied to their lives. The law—expressed through the rules that parents and teachers added to their lives—was not necessarily bad. What *was* bad was that it caused a huge deficit in each child's spirit account.

How do you correct a deficit in an account? Better yet, how do you prevent a deficit in the first place? You make deposits. That's what is missing in our culture and in our children—grace deposits. Grace deposits allow you to build an account so that it does not end up like those of the Columbine killers—in *grace deficit.*

RITE OF PASSAGE PARENTING

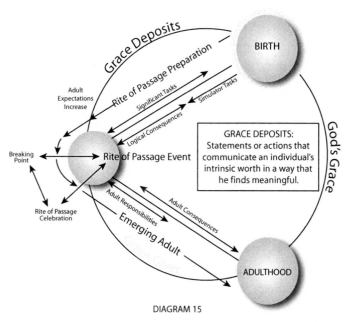

DIAGRAM 15

A child who receives enough grace deposits is able to balance the law under which she lives with plenty of positive messages that communicate her true worth and value. There on the porch, Grandpa Walton lovingly gave John-Boy grace deposits. The students in my youth group listened willingly to the senior adults . . . once those same senior adults made grace deposits into the students' lives. Students and seniors affirmed each other's worth, so they both were making grace deposits, and we didn't have any accounts that were overdrawn.

When we completed the transition from an agricultural to an industrial society and lost, for the most part, the influence of grandparents and other extended family members, our kids also lost grace deposits. Today, our kids are confused by the mixed messages parents send ("You're so special! You drive me crazy! Now go clean up that room!"). In fact, many parents give their children very few grace deposits at all. Because they don't know *how* to put grace into a child's life or into his spirit account, they have a difficult time doing it. Without grace deposits, kids can end up feeling like leftovers.

No Leftovers

When Jeremiah and Caleb lived at home, one of the things that irked me most was when they returned almost empty containers to the refrigerator. In fact, it wouldn't surprise me a bit to find a plastic bowl hiding on one of the shelves, holding one remnant green bean from Thanksgiving 1997. In all of our meal planning since that time, we have never had a need for that lone bean. Nevertheless, it will sit in its place in the bowl on the refrigerator shelf because someday, somehow, somewhere, we might need one green bean.

Food items are not the only leftovers in our world. Today, many children feel like leftovers. No one knows what to do with them, so we wrap them up, shelve them, and shove them to the back of the refrigerator—the place where all leftovers eventually reside. There they sit, waiting for someone to come along, pull them out, and say, "I want you" . . . "I need you."

Satan wants your children to see themselves as leftovers: unusable and unnecessary. Leftover children become leftover adults. People who have a leftover mentality never change the world. They don't feel needed. They don't sense their part in a greater plan. They certainly don't become capable, responsible, self-reliant adults.

In all of his creation, God has never had a single leftover. Every bird, every cloud, every leaf, and every child is a part of his eternal, sovereign plan. The Master of the Universe designed our children to be significant. As parents, our task is to help them see themselves as he sees them. They can only do that if, when they look into our eyes, they can tell that *we* see them as valuable and significant. Our eyes and our words need to reflect the purposes God has for their lives.

When your children look into your eyes, do they see immediately that they are valuable? Significant? Wonderfully made? Or do they see only leftovers?

Families who find ways to build grace deposits into their kids' lives will let them know that they are *not* leftovers. Their kids will gain identity and self-worth because of the investments made in their lives by the people who know and love them. Those are the kind of deposits everyone needs. Those are the kind of deposits that *Rite of Passage Parenting* calls *grace*.

CATHY, THE BASKETBALL MOM

My wife, Cathy, understands grace deposits. In fact, she's an expert on giving them. In order to relate to our oldest son, a sports enthusiast, my wife did something that I found very meaningful. She asked him to help her learn more about professional basketball. Jeremiah gave her a list that included about a dozen of his favorite players and their nicknames. She memorized the entire thing, even though she didn't have a clue about any of these players beforehand.

Now you need to understand that my wife is a petite, blonde Norwegian who loves her family much more than she loves sports. Cathy knew exactly how important basketball was to our son, so she studied Jeremiah's list. She learned that Charles Barkley of the Houston Rockets has a nickname: the Chuck Wagon. Karl Malone of the Utah Jazz is called the Mailman because he *delivers*, and Larry Bird, Jeremiah's all-time favorite, is Larry the Legend.

I have never seen a kid as delighted as Jeremiah, sitting at the kitchen counter and drilling his mom on her memory work. He would bring his friends to the house and beam as she rattled off basketball facts. You could see it on their faces: they were amazed that Jeremiah's mother knew so much about basketball. "Your mom is the coolest," they would say as they left the house.

Now, Cathy didn't care a bit about being cool. What she cared about then is what she cares about now: putting grace deposits into our sons' lives. Every time she memorized a player and his nickname, she was showing Jeremiah how important he was. Through her words and her actions, she was giving him grace deposits. I think she made a slam-dunk.

·∘{ RITE OF PASSAGE PARENTING SUMMARY }∘·

The cultural shift has removed the intergenerational relationships that naturally built grace deposits (statements or actions that communicate an individual's intrinsic worth) into kids' lives. We have moved away from grandparents, many of whom no longer invest in their grandchildren's lives. This has led parents to look outside the family for help in raising their children.

Positive intergenerational relationships meet needs in the lives of both younger and older people. Many of today's rebellious young people have experienced a grace deficit in their spirit accounts. This causes them to feel like leftovers, uncertain about who they really are.

CHAPTER ELEVEN

How It Shows:
"You'll Never Amount
to Anything!"

Our kids fail to achieve capable, responsible adulthood because they have failed to receive correct messages about their identity: an individual's accurate understanding of his or her unique attributes.

B ut go, tell his disciples—and Peter—that he is going before you into Galilee; there you will see him, as he said to you" (Mark 16:7 NKJV).

For a long time, this section of the resurrection story confused me. Why did the angel say "and Peter," anyway? Peter *was* one of the twelve disciples.

Read between the lines of Scripture, and I think you will see how grace deposits played a crucial role in this disciple's story. Peter was the popular disciple—bold, rough-and-ready, willing to die in place of Jesus . . . and the one who wept bitterly after denying him three times. Peter was someone with whom we can identify, because Peter was *normal*. He loved Jesus—but he made mistakes. He served Jesus—but he didn't always have the right answers. He followed Jesus—but when the going got tough, he ran away. We can all relate to Peter.

Let's examine what happened to Peter before the angel

spoke those words that we find so hard to understand. I like to read the same story in different Gospel accounts, so I looked at Luke 22 for the rest of the story. First of all, let me point out that Peter made a *careless commitment*. When Jesus warned him that Satan was planning to attack him, Peter, in what we know was typical Peter style, had an answer ready: "Lord, I am ready to go with you, both to prison and to death" (Luke 22:33 NKJV). He tossed the answer off so easily—and within a few short verses, his life failed to demonstrate its truth. Peter's commitment was careless.

Second, Peter showed a declining devotion to his authority, Jesus. In verse 33, Peter was ready to die for the Master, but just twenty-one short verses later, he followed Jesus to the high priest's house "at a distance" (Luke 22:54 NKJV). Peter wasn't standing beside his Lord in his hour of need. He certainly wasn't ready to go with Jesus to prison and to death—he couldn't even make it past the courthouse steps. We sigh when we read that his *declining devotion* caused him to slip slowly away from his beloved Lord and Master. We sigh especially because we've done the same thing.

Just one verse later, Peter's abandonment of his Lord had progressed to the point that he "sat among them" (Luke 22:55 NKJV). Peter was engaged in fireside conversation with the Roman soldiers who had arrested Jesus. What a perfect, painful setting for his heartbreaking denial of his Lord in the next few verses. What a perfect, painful picture of the progression we make from careless commitment to declining devotion to *eating with the Enemy*.

Peter *did* deny his Lord: not once, not twice, but three times. After the third denial, Scripture says that Jesus "turned and looked at him" (Luke 22:66 NKJV), catching him eye to eye.

I understand just how Peter must have felt. My mother was

a master at communicating an entire life message with a single look. I can remember sitting in a pew at church, wiggling around and chattering with my friends. From her seat in the choir loft, my mother could catch my eye, stop my activity, and cause my entire life to flash before me, all with a single look.

As Peter caught Jesus' eye, I am confident that he immediately took himself out of the picture, assuming his poor choices meant that he could no longer be considered one of the Twelve. He deliberately placed himself on the back shelf because Peter believed he was a leftover.

When the angel said, "Go tell the disciples—and Peter," the two Marys ran to share their news with the disciples. After that, I can picture them hammering excitedly on Peter's door. He sits in the darkness, his head in his hands, thinking aloud, What a schmuck! How could I go from proclaiming my great loyalty to Jesus before my friends to sitting among his enemies and denying him three times? Every bit of life's guilt and bitterness has transferred itself to Peter's spirit account, and the balance rests at a solid zero.

"Peter, Peter!" the two Marys persist. "Peter, we have a word for you. Jesus is alive—the angel sent us to tell you."

"Surely he didn't mean *me*," Peter mumbles. "You must be looking for Peter the butcher—he lives right down the street. Or maybe it was Peter the cobbler—he has a sandal shop around the corner. I know he couldn't have meant me."

At some point, grace broke down the walls Peter erected, and the message filled his spirit account to overflowing. I know this because I see his response in Luke 24:9–12. At first, the Eleven did not believe that Jesus had risen—but one disciple ran immediately to the tomb. You guessed it. The disciple of gloriously renewed faith was Peter.

Jesus used the angel to send Peter the message of the

Marys and a word for each of us. Instead of looking at what Peter did and chastising him, "You'll never amount to anything!" Jesus knew that Peter needed extra grace. Through the message of the Marys, God sent the despondent disciple a huge grace deposit: "I still believe in you. You will see me again. You can follow me."

In traditional Jewish culture, when two people have had a time of distress or disagreement, they come back together by celebrating a restoration meal. Do you remember what Jesus did in John 21? He stood on the bank, cooking a feast of fish for his disciples in the early morning. Which fisherman impetuously removed his robe and jumped out of the boat, ready to share the meal and to follow Jesus anywhere? Again, you guessed it. The beach picnic was Peter's restoration meal. The meal, the words, and the timing were all examples of grace deposits.

That story brings me hope. When I fail, I am thankful that my God is the God of a thousand chances, one who says to me over and over again, "Come back, Walker. Come back to my loving grace."

When we feel graceless, when we are sure that we have no value or worth to anyone because we have messed up so badly, when we feel like leftovers, Jesus sends us the message of the Marys. It is the message of the empty tomb: "Come back! I believe in you! You will see me!" In fact, the empty tomb has two messages. The first tells who Jesus is—the Savior of the World, the Lord of the Resurrection. But the second message is one of grace to those who are his followers . . . even when they fail and fall.

The grace deposit from our Lord brought Peter back where he belonged. In Acts 2:14, he took his stand with the other apostles. What brought Peter the denier, Peter the goof-up, Peter the jerk, back to this place of powerful faith? What allowed him to stand strong once more? What ultimately granted him, as tradition tells us, the honor of dying upside down on a cross for his Lord? I believe it was the message of grace.

Grace Deficit

"But I don't get it, Walker," I can hear you saying. "Jesus put plenty of grace deposits into Peter's life. Why did he choose to walk away?"

The truth is that Peter's story is Caleb's story—and yours, and mine. No, Cathy and I were not perfect parents, but we had instilled right values and right beliefs into our son. We had done what we could to raise him to love God and honor his Word. Why did he walk away? Why do so many other kids do the same thing?

If you look at Peter's life, you will see that he was always trying to be someone he wasn't. This caused him to run away from the grace deposits, never allowing people to affirm who he was. Sometimes, like Caleb and like Peter, our kids are not satisfied with who they are. The sin of unbelief blinds their eyes even to all the right values and right beliefs we have put into their lives. At the same time, Satan whispers lies that become withdrawals from their spirit accounts: "You're no good . . . You'll never amount to anything . . . Who would ever want you? . . . You're a loser!"

Like Peter, today's kids often have empty accounts. Like Peter, they often turn to artificial means of filling them. Peter went very quickly from careless commitment to declining devotion to eating with the Enemy—trying new relationships and activities to fill the void in his life. Thanks to the grace deposits brought through the message of the Marys, he made a very quick turnaround.

Some kids take longer to come home. They keep searching for ways to fill their spirit accounts through false or misleading deposits. Deep inside, the individual always knows his spirit account is empty. That's why *Rite of Passage Parenting* calls these false attempts to fill it *counterfeit grace*.

> ↦ COUNTERFEIT GRACE: False or misleading deposits into a spirit account that cause it to appear full but add no genuine value.

HOW IT SHOWS: PEER DEPENDENCE

Counterfeit grace appears in a variety of forms. One of the most familiar—and frustrating—to parents is the way McDonald's Kids turn to others just like them in search of individual identity.

John-Boy and his brothers and sisters had no trouble with identity. They understood who they were because they knew what they did (simulator tasks and later, significant tasks) and because their parents, grandparents, and other relatives had added plenty of grace deposits to the right values and right beliefs they had already instilled in their lives. After experiencing their rites of passage, they approached capable, responsible, self-reliant adulthood in complete security. When they had questions, they went to their elders. When they had concerns, they went to their elders. When they had problems, they went to their elders. Intergenerational contact gave them grace deposits.

> ↦ IDENTITY: An individual's accurate self-understanding of his God-given, unique attributes.

Today's grandparent-less, graceless generation fears rejection so much that its members feel a strong pressure to conform to the group, says psychologist Ronald Koteskey. The psychological term for this is *peer dependence*.

> Unfortunately, those other teens do not know who they are either, so peer pressure becomes a case of "the blind leading the blind." . . . Such conformity shows in actions, language, beliefs, possessions, and, most obviously, in dress . . . If parents suggest wearing something not "in" with the group at the moment, the suggestion will be met with, "Do I have to wear that?"
>
> Social psychologist Solomon Asch showed that adolescents conform, even to a group of strangers, on such a simple thing as judging which of two lines is longer. When making judgments alone, teens made errors about 7 percent of the time. When judging with a group of three or more people, they made errors about 33 percent of the time if the rest of the group was unanimously against them.
>
> As the differences between the lines became less, the teenagers conformed to the group more. If they were made to feel less competent than the others in the group, they conformed even more. Unfortunately, many of the decisions adolescents make are much less clear-cut than judging the lengths of lines. Since they are also unsure of their identities, they are likely to conform to nearly anything the rest of the group does . . . They look to others to decide how to act because they do not know who they are.[1]

A graceless teenager whose spirit account has zeroed out alienates herself from family relationships. At this point, the teen is most susceptible to the lure of a gang or cult. Both of these subgroups offer the addition of counterfeit grace by providing the teen with the accepting, approving, affirming words and actions she craves. Since these kids either do not get or do not *perceive* that they get adequate grace deposits from their parents and extended family, they seek them elsewhere.[2]

Even a *good* group can cause problems in teens' lives, as Koteskey points out:

> Unfortunately, conformity is not a good answer to identity, even if teens have chosen to conform to a "good" group rather than to a gang. In earlier times, people found lasting identities in their cultures and communities, but these adolescent identities are based on temporary groups. If the group rejects the adolescent, the result can be devastating. When the group breaks up, as nearly all adolescent groups finally do, the adolescent is again left without an identity.[3]

How It Shows: Techno-Grace

Today's world offers young people more and more alternative subgroups that provide ways of adding counterfeit grace to their spirit accounts. One that has received recent notoriety is teens' increasing use of technology—and not just technology but, as a recent *Time* article points out, multitasking technology. The Multitasking Generation describes a world in which parents and teens are so turned-on and tuned-in to their individual computers, iPods, cell phones, and other means of electronic multitasking that they rarely connect in person. "We saw that when the working parent comes through the door, the other spouse and the kids are so absorbed by what they're doing [with technology] that they don't give the arriving parent the time of day."[4]

Counterfeit grace such as that received by the multitasking McDonald's Kids from their various electronic communicators takes up time, energy, and space; consequently, today's young people often don't receive genuine grace deposits even when they're offered. Counterfeit grace even causes its recipients to mistrust the validity of any genuine grace deposits they receive.

No wonder today's young people live in a constant state of grace deficit. Their spirit accounts have been falsely filled with counterfeit grace.

How It Shows: MySpace Grace

MySpace and other adolescent-geared social Internet sites such as Facebook have received recent publicity as the adult world suddenly awakened to their frequently graphic contents and potential for crime. Again, the teens who frequent these sites often do so as a means of receiving counterfeit grace. They post their thoughts and then watch for the response. *Is someone out there reading? Will they validate me? Do they care what I think?*

Although the results may look like grace deposits, they're often far from genuine.

Officials are concerned that teens who use public Web sites to socialize and plan activities are oblivious to the presence of predators.

"Kids are not connecting what they're doing on the computer

with real life," says Parry Aftab, an online safety expert who has advised MySpace. "They do not believe they're accountable."[5]

The Connecticut attorney general's office that investigated MySpace said that its "failure to shield minors" from pornographic images and sexual predators make it "a parent's worst nightmare."[6] A teen who seeks identity primarily through means such as MySpace inadvertently leaves himself open for huge withdrawals from his spirit account.

> Every day, we dress ourselves in a set of clothes that conveys something about our identity—what we do for a living, how we fit into the socio-economic class hierarchy, what our interests are, etc. This is identity production. Around middle school, American teens begin actively engaging in identity production as they turn from their parents to their peers as their primary influencers and group dynamics take hold. . . . The dynamics of identity production play out visibly on MySpace. Profiles are digital bodies, public displays of identity where people can explore impression management.[7]

TRADING GRACES

Trading healthy marital love for hookups. Trading words of affirmation from a relative for a stranger's posting on your blog. Trading family acceptance for gang initiation. Trading a positive way to express one's faith for a prop.

Satan loves to tempt us to accept a cheap substitute for something God has designed. In the area of relationships, he has some very convincing methods of doing so. Remember? Way back in the garden of Eden, he convinced Eve to accept a few bites of a delicious-tasting fruit instead of an eternal relationship with God. She and Adam willfully substituted the temporary for the timeless and the luscious for the life.

Mom and dad, if you don't get a grip on grace, you'll find your children accepting substitutes for you. Dad, if you don't put grace deposits into your daughter, she will find a hormonally imbalanced, knuckle-dragging ape to come along and add counterfeit grace to her life in ways you don't even want to consider.

A young woman who is starving for grace will fall for even the most obvious lies. She'll mistake his casual, "You're beautiful," for committed love. Far too many young women have been involved in wrong relationships because fathers failed to fill their daughters' spirit accounts with grace deposits.

Mom, you're not off the hook, either. Your son will do the same thing if you fail to put your grace into his life. He may become the high school football star who expects a friends-with-benefits relationship with that sweet girl you met at the game. He may become the techno-geek who spends hours online downloading Internet porn.

Kids whose accounts experience a grace deficit trade the truth for a lie. Eventually, they end up like Peter—like Caleb—like each of us, at one time or another. They rebel against their authority, believing that they don't need the protection and direction that living under its covering always brings. In fact, when they make this dangerous substitution, their character collapses.

DECLINING DEVOTION

Remember Peter and his declining devotion? That was the beginning of his trading the truth for a lie as he started to fall away from—and ultimately rebel against—his authority.

For a moment, let's think back to our building analogy. Just like Peter, our kids find it easy to make careless commitments because the construction of their buildings is faulty. God intends their lives to show right values matched with right beliefs. Instead, there is a crack in the foundation or a chink in the walls brought about by wrong values, wrong beliefs, or both. Because of this mismatch of materials, their characters end up sadly in need of repair and realignment.

Little by little, after Peter began the progression of declining devotion, he began to reject Jesus—the authority in his life. He started following him from afar rather than seeking a more intimate involvement. Little by little, he backed away from Christ's authority and rejected his teaching, insight, and influence.

BUILDING PROJECT

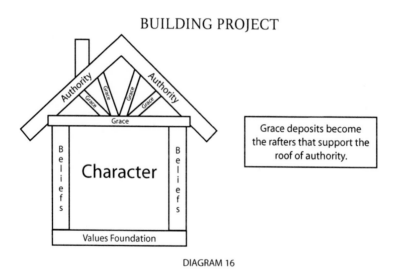

Grace deposits become the rafters that support the roof of authority.

DIAGRAM 16

Think about the building again. God's authority is the roof. Imagine trying to slip the building's foundation and walls out from under his protection. The farther out from under the roof of authority the building slides, the more free access Satan has to your child's life. In a relatively short amount of time, he can damage, even destroy, an entire building. Pretty soon, we see more than just cracks in the foundation and chinks in the walls. We begin to see the entire building collapse. Even if it doesn't fall immediately, it ends up using so many props to support wrong beliefs and wrong values that it is doomed to destruction.

Where do grace deposits fit in with our building analogy? Here, they become the rafters. You see, the rafters not only support the roof, but they also help to hold its walls together. Buildings constructed with the wrong kind of rafters—or not enough of them—display serious problems. Each component of a person's life, each element of the building, is dependent on the others and the support and strength they give. When a child's building doesn't have enough grace rafters to support the roof of authority, he ends up exposed and vulnerable to every storm. Without the rafters, the walls of belief begin to collapse. This building certainly needs help to "fix it, brother!"

⊰ Rite of Passage Parenting Summary ⊱

Peter's denial of Jesus shows a progression that many of today's kids follow because of a genuine or perceived grace deficit in their spirit accounts. Today's kids find many ways to add counterfeit grace to their lives, including peer dependence and multitasking technology such as cell phones and social Internet sites like MySpace or Facebook.

Today's young people have exchanged their true identity for the lies of counterfeit grace, which causes withdrawals from the child's spirit account. In fact, counterfeit grace falsely fills the account, taking the space allotted for grace deposits. Without the identity that grace deposits provide, the child begins to slip away from his authority, missing out on protection and direction. Parents who watch this dismal progression may end up telling their kids, "You'll never amount to anything!"

༄

CHAPTER TWELVE

ESSENTIAL EXPERIENCE #4: ESTABLISH THEIR TRUE IDENTITY THROUGH GRACE DEPOSITS

We need to build true Identity into our kids' lives through our own words and actions and through a specially chosen grace team.

When Caleb and Jeremiah were small, we made an effort to visit their grandparents in Missouri whenever we could. My parents still lived on the farm, and the boys had fun exploring some of my favorite places and engaging in some of my favorite activities. Now I was especially thankful that Mom and Dad had left the inner city. I had no doubt that Caleb would have made a champion tire slasher.

My two city kids loved climbing trees. During one visit, I walked out the front door of my parents' house. Although I don't recall exactly why, I do remember that I was hunting everywhere for my sons. Finally, I spotted them both . . . about twenty feet up in a tree.

In the years since leaving the farm, I had become both a father and a city kid. I wasn't nearly as excited about my sons' tree climbing as I had been about my own bale bucking or fence building.

"Boys!" I said in my best fatherly tone. "Get down from that tree right now!"

"But, Dad—" Once again, it was Caleb's little voice that reached me from the quivering limbs.

"Caleb! Jeremiah! Get down right now! Do you hear me?"

"But, Dad—"

I resigned myself to one more father-son discussion. "Yes, Caleb?"

"What do we do about Grandma?"

"Grandma? What's Grandma got to do with it? Get down out of that tree right now!"

"But, Dad!" Caleb had mastered the art of persistence. "Grandma's up here too."

I craned my neck. There, head cocked, arms and legs wrapped around a branch, was my mother—ten feet higher up in the tree than either of my sons.

Shaking my head, I walked back inside the house, amazed at the grace deposits Mom provided for those boys. She played with them; she laughed with them; she read them stories; she told them how much they meant to her because they were her grandsons. In other words, as far as Caleb and Jeremiah were concerned, Mom made a point of grace. One day not long after that incident, however, Mom had a massive heart attack and died.

A little more than a year before that, Cathy's father had become very ill, and she headed to Missouri to help care for him. For a short time, I took on her role along with my own. Usually, I had a hard enough time just being dad.

One day while Cathy was still taking care of her father, Caleb was too sick to go to school. He seemed to have those days every so often. Since we had just moved to Tulsa for my new position at First Baptist, I wasn't quite sure what to do with my ailing son. Finally, I called a friend from the church and asked for his ideas.

"Do you know Mrs. Hodges?" he asked.

"I'm not sure," I replied. Actually, I thought I knew Mrs. Hodges—but I was sorting through so many new faces and names that I was afraid to guess who she was.

"She's from the church. She recently lost her husband, so I think she may be lonely, and she's really good with kids. Why don't you give her a call? I bet she'd be glad to watch Caleb!"

I got the phone number and, desperate to get to work, decided to call Mrs. Hodges right away. She sounded nice enough, and we quickly agreed that I could drop Caleb off at her home on my way to the church.

I got the report later in the day when I called to check on my youngest son. "Oh, he started turning somersaults across the floor just a few minutes after you left. I think he's fine, Brother Walker. We've been playing games and having snacks— we even made some cookies together! That's quite a boy that you and your wife have there. Quite a boy." I was used to hearing that Caleb was quite a boy, but Mrs. Hodges sounded much kinder than some of the other people who made that comment.

Not long afterward, Cathy's father passed away. When my mother also died, we had lost two grace-giving grandparents in a year's time, but God had a plan to keep our boys' spirit accounts from ending up in grace deficit. Our family kept seeing Mrs. Hodges here and there (by this time, we were calling her by her first name, Lucile), and she kept volunteering to keep our boys. Before long, it made sense to all of us to include her as part of the Moore family. Lucile became an adopted grandma to our sons and, since I had so recently lost my mother, an adopted mom to me. Through the years, she has become one of the strongest encouragers, greatest supporters, and most generous grace depositors our family has ever known. In our family's life, Lucile has always made a point of grace.

Just Checking . . .

Can I ask you to do me a favor? Stop reading this book right now. Before you go on to the next sentence, I have an important learning activity for you. Go get your checkbook, bring it back, get your pen, and open to the next blank check. Write today's date at the top.

Where it says, "Pay to the order of," I want you to write "Walker Moore" (that's *W-A-L-K-E-R M-O-O-R-E*). See that little square over there with the dollar sign in front of it? I want you to write the amount of the check right there. Write in a *1*, then a comma, then three *0*s, then another comma, and three more *0*s.

On the next line of the check, I want you to write out these words: *One million dollars and no cents.* You're almost finished. On the lower right-hand side, just sign your name.

Now take your check, put it in an envelope, and address it to *Walker Moore, Tulsa, Oklahoma.* That's all the address you'll need. (Can you tell that I've been practicing my televangelist skills?)

What do you mean, "I can't do that"?

Sure, you can do that. Anybody can do that.

You see, *writing* a check for a million dollars is not the problem. The problem will occur when I take that check to my bank to cash it. Your bank will tell my bank that you have insufficient funds—that you haven't put in enough deposits to cover such a huge withdrawal.

You see, your bank (and my bank, and every other bank I know about) has a funny little rule: you have to deposit more money than you withdraw. If you fail to do this, your check will bounce.

So what does this have to do with Rite of Passage Parenting? Put down your checkbook now . . . just keep reading.

Essential Experience #4: Adding Grace Deposits

The only thing that bounces higher than a bad check is a child whose spirit account has more withdrawals than deposits. As we saw in chapter 11, graceless kids end up *bouncing* in a number of destructive ways. Mom and dad, if you want to prevent your kids from bouncing, or fix the ones who are already doing so—even the ones like Peter and Caleb who have bounced right out from under the roof of authority—if you want to know how to fix it, brother . . . keep reading!

1. Look at them eye to eye.

How do you give a grace deposit to your kids? First of all, you look at them eye to eye. Kids know that when you look them in the eye, you're paying attention. We all know about *distracted spouse syndrome* ("DSS"). That's the condition in which the eyes never leave the computer monitor or television screen (somehow, many cases of DSS occur during professional sports games), the head nods, and the words come absently, "Yes, dear."

We don't want to extend DSS to our relationships with our kids—or anyone else in our family. A friend of mine had the importance of eye-to-eye contact pointed out to him just the other day. He was watching the Final Four on television as his little daughter tried in vain to speak with him. Finally, in frustration, she stood in front of his easy chair, grabbed him by the chin, turned his face toward her, and said, "Daddy! Listen with your eyes."

The first way we can build our kids' identities through grace deposits is to give them visual contact—to listen with our eyes. Looking at them eye to eye demonstrates that we care, and that adds something special to their spirit accounts. It's called *grace deposits*.

2. USE THEIR NAMES.

Names are important to God. When you are attempting to add grace deposits to your kids' spirit accounts, make certain that you use their names. First of all, the very act of giving someone a name is a mark of lordship, of authority over him or her. It's a sign that says *you belong to me.*

When God made the sun, the moon, and the stars (see Genesis 1), he named them. He was their Creator and Lord. When he created Adam, God gave him the responsibility of naming all the animals, because Adam was the lord over all these animals. When Jesus was born, his earthly father, Joseph, did not get to name him. Instead, his heavenly Father (and, of course, his Lord) had already done so through the angel: "You shall call his name JESUS, for He will save His people from their sins" (Matt. 1:21 NKJV).

When Jesus chose his disciples, he used their names—and he renamed several of them. In the past, these men had negative connotations attached to their names—just as many of us do today. Jesus wanted to be able to look his followers in the eye and say something positive, so he gave them new names that signified who they were and how he felt about them.

Jesus used these new names to tell the disciples that he expected them to do greater things than he did (John 14:12). Simon became "the rock" who, although his declining devotion caused him to turn away for a time, began the church that would change the world. Saul the persecutor became Paul the protector and defender of the faith. Names are important. Names carry worth and value. Names signify grace deposits.

The principle of expectation says that you often grow into what people think you are. If you think they don't expect very much of you, guess what you will become? If you see yourself as a leftover, you wind up in the back of the refrigerator, never chosen for anything.

Jesus did not allow his disciples to keep the *leftover* label. Instead, the new names he gave them showed how much he believed in them. These names were the message of the Marys even before it was sent—saying, "I believe in you. You will follow me. You will see me." When our children experience grace deficits, the one thing that can draw them back is grace.

Mom and dad, I know you are good parents, and it's still not your fault that your kids sometimes do wrong. Our culture has brought so many changes to families' lives that it's a wonder any of us are standing today. You know of my own failures and struggles as a father. What I can tell you today is that, in the same way grace worked in Peter's life and brought him back to his rightful place as one of the Twelve, grace can also work in your child's life—no matter how young or old he is. Use grace deposits to keep your child's spirit account full, and one day, his life will overflow.

3. USE DEPOSIT LANGUAGE.

When you are using your child's name and casting positive expectations into her life, you need to remember something else. Make certain that you use deposit language: *words that add grace deposits to a spirit account.* Don't make the mistake of using words that will cause withdrawals from your child's spirit account when you are intending to make grace deposits. After all, you don't want to get caught giving counterfeit grace.

⤿ DEPOSIT LANGUAGE: Words that add grace deposits to a spirit account.

The best and simplest way I can explain this is to remind you to use the word *because*. Say to your child, "I admire you *because* you helped your sister put on her shoes without anyone asking you."

"Son, I appreciate you *because* you unloaded the dishwasher on your own."

"Daughter, I'm grateful for you *because* you look for ways to make other people smile."

Because words make your grace deposits specific, ensuring that they end up in the right account with the right value attached. Otherwise, a grace deposit can inadvertently end up as a withdrawal.

Generic compliments work just like that. Have you ever been told, "You're so wonderful," or "You're so special!"?

When you hear a generic compliment, what's the first thing you do? I know you do it, because I do the same thing. You immediately think, *Well, I'm not really wonderful. My desk is messy . . . that's not wonderful. They must not know about my desk.* Or you say to yourself, *Special? Ha! They didn't see the way I argued when my wife asked for my help. I know I'm not really special.*

Generic compliments give Satan an opening to whisper lies about who we are and what we do. Use the deposit language of *because* statements to foil his plans by speaking truth into your kids' lives about their identity and about God's desires for their lives. That kind of deposit language helps communicate true grace.

4. JUST DO IT!

In the last few pages, I've made a strong emphasis on what you *say* when you give your kids grace deposits. However, I want to make sure you understand that grace deposits are also what you *do.*

Once again, a story involving one of my sons best explains what I mean. I was speaking about parenting at a fairly large church. Caleb, just a young boy at the time, had gone along for the day. During a break, some of the women of the church cornered him, thinking they would get the inside scoop on Walker Moore.

"So how do you know your dad loves you?" was one of the questions they asked. I know, because I heard the exchange as I came around a corner unexpectedly.

Caleb's sunny grin lit up the hallway. "He *wrestles* with me."

For Caleb, *grace* was spelled w-r-e-s-t-l-i-n-g. As parents know very well, kids are different. Just as my boys have different ways of thinking and acting, they also have different ways of receiving grace deposits. Jeremiah also liked to wrestle, but not nearly as much as he loved having someone listen to him and

GRACE BANKING

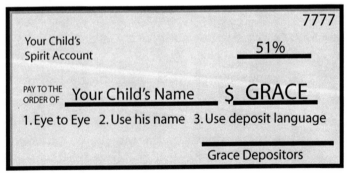

DIAGRAM 17

value the same things he did. When Cathy, the basketball mom, learned about Jeremiah's favorite players, she was using both words and actions to give him grace deposits.

THE GRACE TEAM

Remember Lucile Hodges? She is our family's adopted mom and *designated grace depositor,* and we are grateful for her because she fulfills this role perfectly. When my boys played sports, she attended every game. When I stepped out and began a ministry designed to provide young people with a rite of passage and significant tasks, she stood by my side. Lucile has been there for us in ways we could never have imagined ahead of time, and we've tried to do the same for her.

> ✦ DESIGNATED GRACE DEPOSITOR: Someone chosen to pour grace deposits into a child's life.
> ✦ GRACE TEAM: Those people who can consistently make a positive difference in a child's life through words and actions that affirm, support, and build his true identity.

I did not know Lucile, and I had not yet learned these principles when my sons were born. Today, I encourage you to surround your child—from the day of birth onward—with people who can consistently make a positive difference in his life . . . a grace team. As soon as you know that God is preparing to bless you with a child, begin praying with your mate about whom he intends to place on this child's grace team. This group of people will pour God's grace into your child's life, especially during those many times when mom and dad must be the law.

The Waltons did not have to go looking outside their family for a grace team. The Waltons had each other. Because of our culture's loss of intergenerational relationships, our kids often need numerous designated grace depositors. Some, such as a teacher or coach, will serve temporarily. Others (like Lucile in our family) will form part of your child's grace team, encouraging him through the years. They will also be there to support you, the parents, as you make some of the tough decisions that are always a part of parenting. You'll never regret forming a grace team for your child, and you'll never regret the building up of his or her spirit account through grace deposits.

RITE OF PASSAGE PARENTING

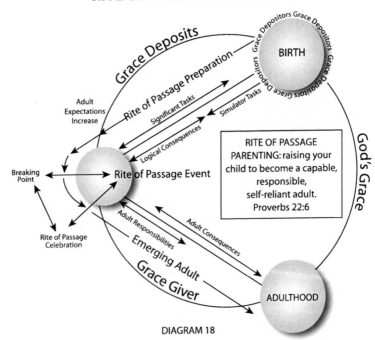

RITE OF PASSAGE PARENTING: raising your child to become a capable, responsible, self-reliant adult. Proverbs 22:6

DIAGRAM 18

Painful Grace

As I watched the police car drive away through the night with my furious son locked inside, I hurt. I hurt for Caleb. I hurt for my wife, who would soon find out that I had allowed her youngest son to go to jail. I hurt for myself—a man who had taught these principles for a number of years and gratefully pointed to his sons as examples of their truth. Even though allowing Caleb to experience logical consequences was right, it was also hard.

Because you are good parents, I'm sure you have figured out by now that at the point at which Caleb went to jail, he was graceless. The choices he made had combined to withdraw all the grace that even the good influence of a godly family and additional grace depositors like Lucile had put into his life. That night, Caleb looked and felt like a leftover.

The next weeks and months became the true test of my teaching. After the police took him away, I went back home and fell to my knees. I said to God, "I've done everything I know to do. I'm far from perfect, but I worked hard trying to raise my boys according to your will and Word. This is the hardest thing for me to do—to let my child experience logical consequences."

I knew that I would experience logical consequences too. That scared me. The Christian world tends to shoot its wounded . . . and that description certainly fit me at the time. I remember saying to Caleb at one point, "What am I gonna do with you, son?" His reply was profound: "I don't know, Dad. *You* wrote the book."

I *did* write the book, and if anyone should have had an answer, it should have been Walker Moore. I knew that this incident might very well place my writing and speaking ministry in serious jeopardy.

I became even more honest with God. "God, I tried to do everything you showed me, and my child still chose to do wrong."

At that moment, I sensed God putting his strong arm around my tired shoulders: *I know. I had the same problem.*

That woke me up. It provided a lot of hope—and a lot of help. Again, God spoke, *Walker, you can't imagine what I did for them. I made them a perfect garden, a place that had everything. I only made one simple little rule—don't eat of just one tree—and they couldn't even follow that. Even though I did everything right, my children still chose to do wrong.*

What I had experienced was no less than what God himself has experienced. Both of us have had children who failed. When his children chose to do wrong, God provided grace . . . and a way to return.

I realized right then that I could either respond in the normal human manner or become like God and continue to put grace into my son, no matter what. Cathy and I began to find ways to give Caleb grace deposits. This didn't necessarily come easily—and at first, Caleb didn't particularly enjoy receiving them. However, I knew that what I saw in Scripture and taught for years must be true: Caleb would only resubmit to us as his authority (and ultimately, to God) if we put enough grace deposits into his life to cover those withdrawals.

Again, I'll allow Caleb to share from his own perspective.

The Rest of Caleb's Story

The real lesson didn't come from just going to jail. Being arrested was not what brought me back to the Lord and to my parents' authority. Many people spend time in correctional facilities without ever encountering true grace. The real example of this came after my dad had insisted on law or, as he would call it, logical consequences.

To help cover the staggering court costs and attorney fees, I had to sell my car. This left me without any way to get around, and I had to use public transportation. Although the bus could take me to work, it could not provide a way home. The buses stopped running around ten at night, but with my job at Blockbuster, I didn't get off until one or sometimes two in the morning.

After all I had put my parents through, they had every right to make me walk home. Instead, each time I finished a shift, my father was there to pick me up. I could tell he was tired and sometimes frustrated, but he never complained or held it over me. Somehow, the fact that he didn't complain was more effective discipline than any reprimand he could have dispensed.

After those late nights, my mother would take her turn for the morning drives. Since the buses hadn't started their routes yet, she would drive me to the city building where I completed my community service time. This became our every-other-day routine for a number of months. I saw Jesus as my mom sacrificed to give me the grace I didn't deserve.

My father did not give me a Sunday school answer. He did not simply tell me that I needed Jesus. He understood what it truly meant to disciple someone—even when that someone did not want to *be* a disciple. I began to see pure faith expressed through love and grace. I began to see past the anger and hate I had expressed to him for sending me to jail that night. I began to see the face of Jesus.

Although their grip was loosening, the drugs and alcohol that had gotten me arrested were still a problem in my life.

One night I failed to come home. I had told my parents that I was going to stay the night at a friend's house and that he would pick me up from work. My friend did pick me up, but we did not go to his apartment. Instead, we binged heavily on beer and shots of alcohol at a nearby bar. Somewhere in the fog of stupid thinking, we decided to take a road trip.

I woke up the next day in Arkansas, about five hours away from home. My head hurt, but the guilt hurt worse. I immediately went to a tattoo shop (tattooing was still illegal in Oklahoma) and got the number thirteen tattooed on the back of my neck in Roman numerals, just like the Johnny Cash song "Thirteen." The meaning was simple: a thirteenth chance at life. I had told myself that I would get that tattoo when I made a final decision to quit drinking.

I arrived home late that afternoon and told my parents what had happened. I had decided it was time to stop fighting and hiding. I showed them the tattoo, and, with tears in my eyes, surrendered: "I submit."

Dad had talked to me many times about the idea of submitting to an authority, but I fought it. Control is something we fight hard to gain—and never really have anyway. I put my broken life into my father's hands and asked him to help me *fix it* (yeah, you could say I grew up on that phrase).

I can honestly say that submitting back to my parents' authority has made all the difference in the world. I had always thought of submitting as giving up. Instead, it was just the opposite. Together, my parents and I would declare war on the pain that I had brought upon myself through my foolish choices.

Raised as the son of a minister and knowing all the politics that can find their way into organized religion, I had a well-earned distrust for anyone who claimed to be a follower of

Jesus. However, the one thing that helped me rediscover my faith was the love of my parents. They had no reason to do the things they did, but they continued to love me back into the arms of God.

Even the love of a parent can be drained by continuous disobedience and extreme bitterness, but the love of the Lord endures forever. I honestly believe that the man who picked me up from work on so many late nights and the woman who drove me all over town on so many early mornings were not my mother and father. Their love had been used up a long time ago. In my opinion, they were relying solely on the strength and love of the God they served. That changed me more than any sermon I have ever heard or any book that I have ever read. Dad may call that grace deposits, but I call it the compelling love of Jesus Christ.

Today I serve the Lord as a youth minister but not because I went to jail and had all those bad experiences. That is not what taught me, nor is it a major part of my testimony today. The real lesson came through the love of my godly parents.

You see, most parents would never do for their child what Mom and Dad did for me. I know because I work with parents every day. Doing what mine did takes the kind of love and knowledge that come only from God. This kind of love bullies its way past all the wrongdoings and opportunities to say "I told you so" and throws its arms around the least-deserving people.

When I speak in public, I often hear the comment, "You sound just like your father." I used to get annoyed by these comparisons. Now, after all we have been through together, I hope that some of his character has rubbed off on me. I know that the goal of both my parents is to echo the love of Christ to those around them. Today, that is my goal as well.[1]

Past Perfect

Caleb was not the only one who learned from this experience. I learned too. I learned what it was to get a couple of hours sleep and then get up again so I could drive downtown in the cold to pick up my son who would sit, sullen and unmoving, huddled in the corner of the passenger's side of my car. I learned what it was to keep offering grace not just by making those drives but also by talking to my son as we rode along—even when he rejected me over and over again.

As God worked through me to pour grace into Caleb's life, I realized that grace really does cover all. I could not give my kids a rite of passage without grace. I could not give them significant tasks without grace. I could not allow them to experience logical consequences properly without grace.

Those grace rafters pictured in diagram 16 really did support and hold everything together. Ultimately, that grace moved Caleb to resubmit himself to me as his authority and allowed us to work together to see his life rebuilt.

I also learned something else. Earlier, when I taught about the spirit account and the need for grace deposits, I left out one important principle. You see, certain kinds of accounts earn more than what you put into them. These accounts add to the deposits with what bankers call *interest.* Interest-bearing accounts end up with a balance greater than the sum of their deposits.

When I watch Jeremiah and Caleb today, I see not just the grace deposits but also the interest on the years of investment that Cathy and I and so many others have made. In fact, their lives have a value that far exceeds anything Walker Moore ever deposited there. That's because God's grace is greater than anything I could have asked or thought. His grace has increased my small investment exponentially . . . even though I often fail to do what's right.

You see, Rite of Passage Parenting is *not* about being a perfect parent. If it were, I wouldn't qualify. When I teach, I often have people ask me, "Walker, do you *always* practice what you preach? Did you *always* give your kids logical consequences? Did you *always* offer them significant tasks? And grace deposits— did you extend those at every single opportunity?"

Once again, you know the answer. My wife and sons would be the first to tell you that I am far from the perfect parent. One of the great things about Rite of Passage Parenting is that you only have to institute its principles 51 percent of the time. I tell people that kids are great mathematicians. If you have any doubt about that, watch what happens when you try splitting a candy bar between three of them.

Your kids will know whether you apply significant tasks, or logical consequences, or grace deposits *more often than not.* That's 51 percent of the time. Rite of Passage Parenting covers and contains all of these events—but if you had looked into the Moore house while Caleb and Jeremiah still lived at home, you would not have seen it operating perfectly twenty-four hours a day, seven days a week. We are far from perfect . . . but as Caleb's story shows, we serve a perfect God who can help us go beyond ourselves to reflect his grace.

Rite of Passage Parenting is not about perfect kids any more than it is about perfect parents. In fact, I am not interested in teaching anyone to raise perfect *kids.* My goal—and I hope that by now it is yours as well—is to produce capable, responsible, self-reliant *adults* who are equipped for life. For the past thirty years, I have built my ministry around this goal. I've seen it bear fruit, not just in the lives of my sons but in the lives of the thousands of young people who have served with Awe Star Ministries.

The Rite of Passage Parenting principles are predictable. If you give your kids a rite of passage, they will lay down their adolescence and become emerging adults. If you provide them with significant tasks, they will develop the skills for capable living. If you apply logical consequences, they will build their lives on right values and right beliefs. Finally, if you pour grace deposits into them, they will submit to you as authority and find their true identity in Christ, becoming the capable, responsible, self-reliant adults God designed them to become.

If you would like to provide your child with a genuine rite of passage through a ministry that instills these principles in kids' lives and provides tools for parents to continue the process, please contact Awe Star Ministries using the information below. We'll be glad to serve you because we're dedicated to equipping your kids . . . for life.

AWE STAR MINISTRIES
P.O. BOX 470265
TULSA, OKLAHOMA 74147-0265
1-800-AWESTAR
www.awestar.org

⋅⋅◦[RITE OF PASSAGE PARENTING SUMMARY]◦⋅⋅

Families whose extended family is unwilling or unable to provide kids with grace can benefit from designated grace depositors. These people willingly pour grace deposits into kids' lives. Parents should also prayerfully choose a grace team who will consistently make a difference in their child's life through words and actions that affirm, support, and build his or her true identity. The grace team will also stand alongside the parents throughout the child-rearing process.

Grace depositors—whether parents or others—can provide kids with grace by using deposit language rather than generic compliments, using their names, and *acting* as well as *speaking* grace. Grace deposits can help bring rebellious children back under their parents' authority. Grace is the ultimate key to Rite of Passage Parenting, a process that helps develop capable, responsible, self-reliant adults by equipping them for life.

RITE OF PASSAGE PARENTING GLOSSARY

ADOLESCENCE: A culturally defined term describing the period between childhood and adulthood where an individual is neither a child nor an adult.

ADULT ACTIVITIES: Actions that identify an individual as an adult according to personal or cultural norms.

ADULT CONSEQUENCES: Predictable outcomes determined by one's own choices.

ADULT RESPONSIBILITIES: An individual's obligations to himself and to others under his authority.

ADULTISM: According to educator Stephen Glenn, "any time an adult forgets what it is like to be a child and then expects, demands, and requires of the child, who has never been an adult, to think, act, understand, see, and do things as an adult."[1]

AUTHORITY: A designated person or persons to whom an individual voluntarily submits his will.

B2BS OR BACK-TO-BEDROOM KIDS: Jobless or underemployed Boomerangs who have returned to their parents' homes to live.

BELIEFS: Thoughts expressed as actions.

BOOMERANG GENERATION (ALSO "BOOMERANGS"): Young adults who refuse to be self-reliant and keep returning to their authority for the basic needs of life.

BREAKING POINT: The point at which scientists use the combined acceleration and new gravitational pull of a spacecraft to reset its course.

CHARACTER: Moral core that defines an individual's identity.

CHECKBOOK THEORY: Parents can systematically and positively affirm their children through grace deposits into an inner spirit account.

COUNTERFEIT GRACE: False or misleading deposits into a spirit account that cause it to appear full but add no genuine value.

Deposit Language: Words that add grace deposits to a spirit account.

Designated Grace Depositor: Someone chosen to pour grace deposits into a child's life.

Emerging Adults: Young people who have experienced a rite of passage and gradually assume adult responsibilities and adult consequences.

False Rite of Passage: An artificial means of marking the line between childhood and adulthood.

Friends with Benefits: Bond characterized by the provision of sexual favors for one another without the complications of a romantic relationship.

Grace: Statements or actions that help build a child's sense of self-worth and value.

Grace Deficit: State in which an individual's spirit account has had more withdrawals than grace deposits so that he sees himself as worthless and insignificant.

Grace Deposits: Statements or actions that communicate an individual's intrinsic worth and value in a way that he finds meaningful.

Grace Team: Those people who can consistently make a positive difference in a child's life through words and actions that affirm, support, and build his true identity.

Helicopter Parents: Moms and dads who hover above their children because they don't think the kids are capable of handling things on their own.

Hookups: An even more impersonal bond than "friends with benefits," characterized by the provision of sexual favors with little or no emotional involvement.

Identity: An individual's accurate self-understanding of his God-given, unique attributes.

Informal Rite of Passage: A distinction between childhood and adulthood marked by adult responsibilities and adult consequences rather than formal recognition through an event and/or celebration.

INNOCENCE: Purity in body, mind, soul, and spirit.

LAW: Statements or actions that lessen a child's sense of self-worth and value.

LOGICAL CONSEQUENCES: The predictable outcomes of an action.

LOGICAL CONSEQUENCES CONTRACT: A written document that matches an action(s) to right values and/or right beliefs and specifies its predictable outcomes.

LOSS OF INNOCENCE: Corruption of one or more aspects of purity in body, mind, soul, or spirit.

LUNAR SLINGSHOT: A scientific phenomenon that uses the gravitational pull of the moon to accelerate a spacecraft's momentum and recast its trajectory in a new direction; also known as *gravity assist.*

McDAVID'S TEENS: Young people whose lives demonstrate that they are moving toward capable, responsible, self-reliant adulthood.

McDONALD'S KIDS: Young people who continue to exhibit childish incompetence, irresponsibility, and dependence on others.

NONVALUABLE: Deemed unworthy or unimportant.

PENDULUM OF ADULT RESPONSIBILITY: The point at which an individual assumes adult responsibilities (the obligations of an individual for his own life and for others over whom he has authority.)

PENDULUM OF PHYSICAL MATURITY: The point at which an individual becomes capable of biological reproduction.

PRINCIPLE OF EXPECTATION: Thoughts and ideas planted in an individual's mind that help guide his future development.

PROPS: Statements of false thinking or faulty logic used to justify wrong beliefs or wrong values.

PSEUDO-SIGNIFICANT TASKS: Activities that outwardly appear to be meaningful but have no intrinsic value.

RITE OF PASSAGE: A clearly defined line that distinguishes childhood from adulthood. Includes the following four components:

Rite of Passage Preparation: A series of incremental tasks designed to build adult responsibilities into an individual's life, preparing him for the transition from childhood to responsible adulthood.

Rite of Passage Event: A step that moves an individual quickly and definitely from childhood to adulthood.

Rite of Passage Celebration: A formal recognition by family and friends that acknowledges the crossing over of the line between childhood and adulthood.

Emerging Adulthood: State in which young people have experienced a rite of passage and gradually assume full adult responsibilities and adult consequences.

RITE OF PASSAGE PARENTS: Parents who lead their child toward capable, responsible, self-reliant adulthood by providing ways to bring closure to childhood and experience a rite of passage.

SIGNIFICANT TASK: A special assignment that demonstrates an individual's worth to the people he considers important.

SIMULATOR TASKS: Sequential, developmental activities that build skills for living and prepare the one who performs them for significant tasks.

SPIRIT ACCOUNT: A space within each individual from which he draws self-esteem and self-worth.

SPIRIT OF ENTITLEMENT: An individual's belief that he is owed money, time, possessions, etc. as a function of mere existence: "I am; therefore you owe me."

TEENSPEAK: Coded language used by the teenage subgroup as a means of empowerment.

VALUABLE: Deemed worthy, prized.

VALUES: The things that an individual deems worthy or prizes.

NOTES

INTRODUCTION: WHAT'S WRONG WITH OUR KIDS ANYWAY?
1. The Barna Group, Ltd., "Twentysomethings Struggle to Find Their Place in Christian Churches," www.barna.org.

CHAPTER ONE—WHAT'S MISSING: KIDS NEED A RITE OF PASSAGE
1. H. Stephen Glenn and Jane Nelsen, *Raising Self-Reliant Children in a Self-Indulgent World: Seven Building Blocks for Raising Capable Young People* (Roseville, CA: Prima Publishing, 2000.), x.
2. Ibid., 6.
3. Edith M. Stern, "Denver Students Learn Movie Making in the Classroom," *Popular Science* (April, 1941): 228.
4. Thomas Hine, *The Rise and Fall of the American Teenager* (New York: Avon Books, 1999), 4.
5. Ibid., 5–6. See also J. M. Tanner, *A History of the Study of Human Growth,* (Cambridge: Cambridge University Press: 1981).
6. Ibid., 11.
7. Frederica Mathewes-Green, "Against Eternal Youth," *First Things*, 155 (August–September 2005): 10.
8. "The Significance of the Day," *Bar Mitzvah/Bat Mitzvah and Jewish Resource and Planning Guide,* Milestone Media Group, www.bnaimitzvahguide.com/barmitzvah.php.

CHAPTER TWO—HOW IT SHOWS: "WHY CAN'T YOU JUST GROW UP?"
1. Adapted from Ronald Koteskey, *Understanding Adolescence* (Wheaton: Victor Books, 1987; revised electronic edition, Koteskey, 2005), 15.
2. Koteskey, *Understanding Adolescence* (2005), 16.
3. Adapted from Koteskey, *Understanding Adolescence* (1987), 20.
4. David Alan Black, *The Myth of Adolescence: Raising Responsible Children in an Irresponsible Society* (Yorba Linda, CA: Davidson Press, 1999), 19.
5. Koteskey, *Understanding Adolescence* (2005), 7–8.
6. Ibid., 11.
7. Adapted from Koteskey, *Understanding Adolescence* (1987), 20.
8. Pamela Paul, "The Permaparent Trap," *Psychology Today* (September–October 2003), 36–50.
9. Ibid.
10. Sue Shellenbarger, "Helicopter Parents Now Hover at the Office," The Wall Street Journal Online (March 17, 2006), www.careerjournal.com/columnists/workfamily/20060317-workfamily.html.

11. Linda Gordon and Susan Shaffer, *Mom, Can I Move Back in with You?* (New York: Jeremy P. Tarcher/Penguin, 2005), 203.

12. Paul, "The Permaparent Trap," 42.

13. Lev Grossman, "Grow Up? Not So Fast," *Time* (January 24, 2005): 44.

CHAPTER THREE—ESSENTIAL EXPERIENCE #1: MARK THEIR MATURITY THROUGH A RITE OF PASSAGE

1. European Space Agency, "Let Gravity Assist You," www.esa.int/esaCP/SEMXLE0P4HD_index_0.html.

2. Brent Higgins Jr., e-mail correspondence to Brent and Deanna Higgins, June 30, 2004.

3. Brent Higgins Jr., Xanga weblog (October 11, 2004), www.xanga.com/DeadSilence7.

CHAPTER FOUR—WHAT'S MISSING: KIDS NEED SIGNIFICANT TASKS

1. Hine, *Rise and Fall*, 24.

2. Personal interview, Fred Bootle, Folly Beach, South Carolina, February 12, 2006.

3. Glenn and Nelsen, *Raising Self-Reliant Children*, 1.

4. Jane Adams, *When Our Grown Kids Disappoint Us* (New York: Free Press, 2003), 28–29.

5. Tom Brokaw, *The Greatest Generation* (New York: Random House, 1998), xx–xxi.

CHAPTER FIVE—HOW IT SHOWS: "YOU CAN'T DO THAT— YOU'RE JUST A KID!"

1. Glenn and Nelsen, *Raising Self-Reliant Children*, xii.

2. Gordon and Shaffer, *Mom, Can I Move Back In?*, 152.

3. Glenn and Nelsen, *Raising Self-Reliant Children*, 75.

4. Ibid.

5. Claudia Wallis, "The Multitasking Generation," *Time*, March 27, 2006, 50.

6. "Overstuffed: Eating Out Can Blindside Us," *PSA Rising* (September 27, 2004), www.psa-rising.com/eatingwell/menu_info00903.htm.

7. Hara Estroff Marano, "Rocking the Chair of Class," *Psychology Today* (September-October 2005), 56.

CHAPTER SEVEN—WHAT'S MISSING: KIDS NEED LOGICAL CONSEQUENCES

1. Betsy Hart, *It Takes a Parent: How the Culture of Pushover Parenting Is Hurting Our Kids—And What to Do About It* (New York: G. P. Putnam's Sons, 2005), 24.

Chapter Eight—How It Shows: "What Were You *Thinking?*"

1. Hart, *It Takes a Parent,* 17.
2. "The Blue Tube: Foul Language on Prime Time Network TV," Parents Television Council, www.parentstv.org/PTC/publications/reports/stateindustrylanguage/exsummary.asp.
3. Ibid.
4. Casey Williams, "MTV Smut Peddlers: Targeting Kids with Sex, Drugs and Alcohol," Parents Television Council, www.parentstv.org/ptc/publications/reports/mtv2005/exsummary.asp.
5. Dr. Peter Whybrow, "Spoiled, Entitled, Materialistic Kids," www.connectwithkids.com/products/affluenza.shtml.
6. Hart, *It Takes a Parent,* 130.
7. Jon J. Gallo and Eileen Gallo, "Adult Children and Money," *Probate & Property* (September–October 2004), www.abanet.org/rppt/publications/magazine/2004/so/GalloGallo.html.
8. Gallo and Gallo, "Adult Children and Money."
9. Hart, *It Takes a Parent,* 44–45.
10. George Barna, *Transforming Children Into Spiritual Champions* (Regal, 2003), 20.
11. Ibid.
12. Benoit Denizet-Lewis, "Friends, Friends with Benefits, and the Benefits of the Local Mall," *New York Times Magazine* (May 30, 2004), www.nytimes.com/2004/05/30/magazine.

Chapter Nine—Essential Experience #3: Build Their Discernment Through Logical Consequences

1. Glenn and Nelsen, *Raising Self-Reliant Children,* 67.
2. Hart, *It Takes a Parent,* 154.
3. Josh McDowell, *Why Wait: What You Need to Know about the Teen Sexuality Crisis* (San Bernardino: Here's Life Publishers, 1989), 79.
4. Caleb Moore, e-mail correspondence, April 13, 2006.

Chapter Ten—What's Missing: Kids Need Grace Deposits

1. Glenn and Nelsen, *Raising Self-Reliant Children,* 5.
2. "Building a Relationship with Your Grandchildren," Family First (2004) www.familyfirst.net/famlife/grandkidrelationship.asp.
3. Glenn, *Raising Self-Reliant Children,* 8.
4. Hilary Stout, "Family Matters: Hiring Someone Else to Potty-Train

Your Kids, Teach Them to Ride a Bike," *Wall Street Journal*, Eastern edition (March 31, 2005), D4, www.contemporaryfamilies.org/media/news%20120.htm.

5. Hon. Bill Owens, April 14, 2000, Heritage Lecture #4, "A Year After Columbine: How Do We Heal a Wounded Culture?" The Heritage Foundation, www.heritage.org/Research/Family/hl662.cfm.

CHAPTER ELEVEN—HOW IT SHOWS: "YOU'LL NEVER AMOUNT TO ANYTHING!"

1. Koteskey, *Understanding Adolescence* (2005), 44–45.
2. Eagan Hunter, "Adolescent Attraction to Cults," *Adolescence* (Fall, 1998), www.findarticles.com/p/articles/mi_m2248/is_131_33/ai_53368534.
3. Koteskey, *Understanding Adolescence* (2005), 46.
4. Wallis, "The Multitasking Generation," 50.
5. Janet Kornblum, "Social Websites Scrutinized," *USA Today* (posted February 12, 2006), www.usatoday.com/tech/news/internetprivacy/2006-02-12-myspace-predators_x.htm.
6. Ibid.
7. Danah Boyd, "Identity Production in a Networked Culture: Why Youth Heart MySpace," American Association for the Advancement of Science (February 19, 2006), www.danah.org/papers/AAAS2006.html.

CHAPTER TWELVE—ESSENTIAL EXPERIENCE #4: ESTABLISH THEIR TRUE IDENTITY THROUGH GRACE DEPOSITS

1. Caleb Moore, e-mail correspondence, April 20, 2006.

RITE OF PASSAGE PARENTING GLOSSARY

1. Glenn and Nelsen, *Raising Self-Reliant Children*, 67.

RITE OF PASSAGE PARENTING
STUDY GUIDE

CHAPTER ONE

༄

WHAT'S MISSING:
KIDS NEED A RITE OF PASSAGE

1. How would you describe the "normal" child?

2. Refer to the information at the bottom of page 9. Do you prefer to raise McDavid's Teens or McDonald's Kids? Explain your response.

3. What in your life separated childhood from adulthood?

4. What meaningful contributions to your family life can your children make?

5. What evidences of responsibility would you like to see in your child?

6. How can you encourage your child to be more responsible?

⌒

CHAPTER TWO

How It Shows:
"Why Can't You Just Grow Up?"

1. Is it easy to let your children make adult decisions and experience adult consequences? Why or why not?

2. Why was Jesus' decision to stay in Jerusalem not a sin?

3. When do you think you became an adult?

   Is your perception based on the physical process or the point at which you started having adult responsibilities? Explain your response.

4. How will you know that your children are adults?
   ___ when they move out of the house
   ___ when they pay their own bills
   ___ when they are no longer dependent on me
   ___ when they can make decisions and live with the consequences
   ___ all of the above
   ___ other: _____

5. What artificial rites of passage have you created?

   What artificial rites of passage do you see your children creating?

6. What is the danger of being a "helicopter parent"?

CHAPTER THREE

༄

ESSENTIAL EXPERIENCE #1: MARK THEIR MATURITY THROUGH A RITE OF PASSAGE

1. Do you spend more time trying to prepare your children for adulthood or trying to preserve their childhood? Why?

2. What adult expectations are you communicating to your children? If none, why?

3. Review the list of possible rite of passage events on page 57. What are some events that might serve this purpose for your children?

4. Read 1 Timothy 4:12. What are the five key marks that help us prepare a child for a rite of passage?

5. What can you do to help your child communicate as an adult?

6. How can you lead your children to behave as responsible, respectful adults?

7. How are you modeling unselfish love for your children and teaching them to do the same?

8. To what do you expect your children to surrender? How does that compare to commitment?

9. What are you doing to safeguard the moral purity of your home?

〜

CHAPTER FOUR

What's Missing:
Kids Need Significant Tasks

1. As you think back on your life, what significant tasks were you given?

2. What does your child do that demonstrates his or her worth and adds value to your family?

3. If what we do defines who we are, then who are your children?

4. What significant tasks are you allowing your children to do?

5. Do you believe that giving your children significant tasks is important to them living peaceful, contented, and abundant lives? Why or why not?

6. What are some pseudo-significant tasks in which your children are engaging? What is the danger of them being involved in these activities?

⤳

CHAPTER FIVE

How It Shows:
"You Can't Do That—You're Just a Kid!"

1. How does our performance of the significant tasks God has assigned affect other people? If we don't carry out our tasks, who will take our place?

2. In what ways do your children exhibit their need to be needed?

   How do you usually respond?
   ___ I give them something to do
   ___ I redirect them to something they might enjoy
   ___ I chastise them for bothering me
   ___ I ignore them
   ___ other: _____

3. Compare your childhood to that of your children. What did your parents do for you that you outsource for your children?

4. Who is responsible for the spiritual development of your children?
   ___ the school
   ___ the media
   ___ the church
   ___ the government
   ___ parents

5. How will your approach to significant tasks affect the way your children approach significant tasks when they are older?

⤴

CHAPTER SIX

ESSENTIAL EXPERIENCE #2: EXTEND THEIR LIFE SKILLS THROUGH SIGNIFICANT TASKS

1. What are some specific tasks that your children can perform for your family?

2. What are some simulator tasks that you can use to train your children?

3. What are some necessary life skills that you can teach your children over the next three years? List progressive steps toward those skills. Use the *model, instruct, work alongside,* and *let them do it* process described on pages 117–18.

   What obstacles might you encounter in teaching these skills?

4. Think back on some of the tasks you learned as a child. What process was used in teaching those tasks?

5. What is the spiritual application of this process?

   Do you think today's younger generation will be more or less inclined toward spiritual matters than your generation? Explain your response.

CHAPTER SEVEN

WHAT'S MISSING:
KIDS NEED LOGICAL CONSEQUENCES

1. When your child makes a mistake, are you more likely to . . .
   ___ step in and help avoid the consequences?
   ___ allow your child to face the logical consequences?

   Explain your reasoning.

2. Read 2 Thessalonians 3:10. What is the lesson of this verse?

3. Reflect on your life. What are some of the lessons you have learned from having to face logical consequences?

4. What process was used in your life to teach you how to make good decisions and choices?

   How does the process you are using with your children compare to the process used with you?

5. Read Genesis 2:17 and identify the logical consequence stated in that verse.

   How are we still affected by the decision in the garden to make a bad choice?

6. Review the diagram on page 138. What are the basic beliefs you are instilling in your children?

What will be the resulting character that is developed within these beliefs?

CHAPTER EIGHT

How It Shows:
"What Were You Thinking?"

1. What is the difference between *values* and *beliefs*?

   What are some of your values?

   What are some of your beliefs?

2. How are you instilling values and beliefs in your children?

3. What are some things you can do to guard against your children using props to rationalize bad choices? See page 145 for a definition of *props*.

4. How do you teach the difference between valuable and nonvaluable language?

5. How do you model a proper attitude toward possessions?

6. What are three things you are doing to help your children learn to handle finances?

7. How are you instilling biblical values toward sexuality?

   What are the sources of opposition to these values?

   What should you do about this opposition?

CHAPTER NINE

༤

Essential Experience #3:
Build Their Discernment Through
Logical Consequences

1. Is it more painful to spend your parenting years fixing
   your children's lives or enforcing the logical consequences
   of their actions?

   What do children learn from each approach?

2. What is one logical consequence contract you can establish with your children?

   Issue:

   Logical consequence:

3. Briefly describe one way you might use the *Good Word/Bad
   Word Project* with your children.

4. Briefly describe a *Possessions Contract* you might use.

5. Describe a *Finances Contract* you might use in raising your
   children.

6. What are some elements you would like to see your child
   include in a *Sexuality Contract*?

〜

CHAPTER TEN

WHAT'S MISSING: KIDS NEED GRACE DEPOSITS

1. On the line below place an X indicating your parental style.

   Law ——————————————————————— Grace

2. Describe a time when you have been engaged in inter-generational sharing.

   How do you rate that overall experience?
   ___ positive
   ___ negative

3. Compare and contrast your relationship with your grandparents to the relationships your children have with their grandparents. What is the same? What is different?

4. List three ways you can make grace deposits in the lives of your children.

5. How can you make your children feel significant and valued?

   Why is this so difficult to do?

6. Who made grace deposits in your life? How did those deposits affect you?

CHAPTER ELEVEN

〜

How It Shows:
"You'll Never Amount to Anything!"

1. When your children let you down, how do you respond?

   How does your response compare to the grace and forgiveness demonstrated by Jesus?

2. What is filling your spirit right now?

   What do you think is filling the spirits of your children?

3. How would you describe your children's relationships with their closest peers? Are they followers or leaders? Explain your response.

4. Identity is an individual's accurate self-understanding of his God-given, unique attributes. Write your identity.

   Now write the identities of your children.

   What can you do to reinforce the identities of your children?

5. For what do your children visit mySpace and Facebook? If you visit those sites, what are you seeking?

   How are these sites providing counterfeit grace?

6. What is one thing you can do today to show grace to each of your children?

CHAPTER TWELVE

∽

Essential Experience #4: Establish Their True Identity Through Grace Deposits

1. Who are those people who are making grace deposits in the lives of your children?

2. Make a list of the grace deposits and grace withdrawals your children have experienced this week.

   Now check the balance. Are your children overdrawn? If so, how is that manifesting itself in their behavior?

3. Why is it important to have *designated grace depositors* on your grace team?

4. What have been the most difficult situations in which you have demonstrated grace?

   What has been the most difficult situation in which you have allowed your child to experience the consequences of his or her actions?

5. In a statement or two, sum up what you have learned in this study.

How will the lessons in this study affect your parenting now and in the future?

www.ropparenting.com

You're a good parent who cares about your kids, so I encourage you to visit the *Rite of Passage Parenting* (ROPP) Web site where you'll find a variety of tools to guide you as a Rite of Passage Parent.

····◆····

▶▶ **ROPP MEMBERSHIP:** access to supplemental ROPP materials, free of charge.

▶▶ **ROPP STORE:** the *rite* place to order additional books, other ROPP materials, and the *Rite of Passage Parenting Workbook* (Thomas Nelson, 2007) designed to help you personalize ROPP and *fix it* for your own family. Recommended for a small group setting, the *Rite of Passage Parenting Workbook* can also be used independently by individuals or couples.

▶▶ **ROPP VIDEO:** downloadable vidcasts containing Bible teaching from Dr. Walker Moore. These vidcasts, matched to each session of the *Rite of Passage Parenting Workbook*, support and supplement the ROPP principles.

▶▶ **ROPP DOWNLOADS:** visuals, diagrams, Facilitators' Helps, and additional Fix-It forms for the *Rite of Passage Parenting Workbook* along with a PowerPoint presentation for teaching the ROPP basics.

▶▶ **ROPP DEVOTIONS:** weekly devotions written to encourage you as a Rite of Passage Parent.

▶▶ **ROPP EVENTS:** link to opportunities specifically designed to provide your child with a rite of passage event, available through Awe Star Ministries.

▶▶ **ROPP TALK:** opportunities to interact with other Rite of Passage Parents.

▶▶ **ROPP REVIEW:** space for your personal assessment of the book and/or workbook.

▶▶ **ROPP CONTACT INFORMATION:** schedule and contact information for the teaching ministry of Walker Moore; ways to have Walker or another ROPP/Awe Star representative speak to your church or organization.

For a more detailed, practical application of the
Rite of Passage Parenting Principles suitable for
small group or individual study, check out the
Rite of Passage Parenting Workbook, available online
at www.amazon.com, www.christianbook.com,
or wherever Christian books are sold.

••••●●●••••

For further information including vidcasts of Dr. Walker
Moore's teaching matched with each workbook session,
visit our Web site at www.ropparenting.com.

CPSIA information can be obtained at www.ICGtesting.com
225709LV00005B/1/P

9 780785 289579